SUCCESS
ON YOUR
OWN
TERMS

6 Promises to Fire Up Your Passion, Ignite Your Career, and Create an Amazing Life

James B. Rosseau, Sr.

FOREWORD BY BILLY DEXTER, PARTNER, HEIDRICK & STRUGGLES

"I've never met another colleague in my 25 year business career who draws people in faster than James Rosseau. At first you're struck by his genuine interest in helping you solve your issue, objective, or related conundrum with remarkable clarity. Ultimately, however, you realize he didn't solve your need, but instead subtly did something far more valuable: he gave you the tools and insight to do so yourself. Accountability comes to mind when I think about James—accountability to deliver against business objectives, of course, but more importantly, accountability to yourself: your word, your vision, your life. I think James may have found the secret to success, and it's remarkably simple: Have a plan for your life. And then go get it."

—Dale Rife, vice president, JPMorgan Chase

"The first time you meet James Rosseau you know that he is a special leader. As a manager, James has always led by example by merging strong career management skills with strategic thinking, relationship management, and hard work. As a mentor, he has always offered a perspective that is profound yet simple to execute. Over the nearly 10 years that I have known James, he has always had a clear vision of where he wanted to be, and how to achieve personal and professional balance. For today's professional, this is the new age of how many of us are now beginning to define success. The principles that James has used to manage his own career have become the practices of many of his protégés. Much of our success can be traced back directly to Mr. Rosseau's influence."

—David Brown, director of process management, Deloitte Consulting

"During the time that James and I worked together, it was obvious that he was a sought-after leader. In addition to leading by example, James consistently demonstrates a passion to contribute to the personal and professional success of those around him. His leadership courage to provide candid feedback, coupled with his good intentions, sets him apart from others. I am always interested in hearing about the practical recommendations provided by James, and you will be."

—Joan Verbonitz Frank, vice president, senior HR business partner at Wells Fargo

"I am more than willing to endorse James as someone credible to speak on the topic of work and success. James was my manager for the majority of my career at JP Morgan. He challenged me on a daily basis, provided feedback for development and growth, and continued to inspire me to be a better manager, friend, and father. To this day, I still use the practical advice James has provided to me in the past."

—Steve Mariotti, SVP, Bank of America

"I have worked with James for more than 5 years. He is the most unique and dynamic leader I have worked for in my 21-year career in financial services. From my very first meeting with James, I was able to sense that he was passionate about his career and professional success, while wanting to get to know me better as an individual. As time went by, I realized that this was all part of the bigger picture with James. He was focused not only at being successful within his career, but helping develop people, and show them a path to professional and personal success through individual development. A large part of this individual development is driven through feedback, which James preaches is a gift. James has always been able to provide feedback, both positive and negative, in a way that can be embraced and reflected upon without trepidation. On a personal level, I hold the utmost respect for James. I know the area of Philadelphia that James comes from, and it takes a special person to rise above the negative influences within that setting. Most people aren't able to make it out; they are swept up by those influences. James embraced personal development, and held himself accountable at an early age and that allowed him to rise above. Embracing personal development and accountability remain common threads in his professional management style today. James' background is also a significant reason for his willingness to give back to the community. James has frequently spoke about how he feels the need to leverage his professional success for the greater good. He, more than anyone else I know, is true to his word in this regard."

—Chuck Rosenberry, SVP, business development,
Allstate Affinity Solutions

"I still remember the first day I met Mr. Rosseau. He was walking toward his big, beautiful, cherry wood, sun-drenched office and my cube happened to be right outside his door. I remember the big smile and the simple introduction–just his name and which business unit he was a part of. No mention of his title. Of course I knew he had a significant role in the organization, but it was at that moment I knew I wanted to work with that guy. Through the years, James has served as my and many others' unofficial mentor, willingly making time to listen and offer his perspective. He respects everyone and what they do, no matter how big or small, and never lets his title get in the way of his interactions with the little guys. When James uses the phrase, 'empower your people,' he means it and actually walks the walk, which, in my opinion, puts him in the minority among so-called leaders. He's one of the most down to earth and genuine people I know. James's life journey and the decisions he's made along the way make him a perfect role model for people of all ages and walks of life. I consider myself privileged to be a part of his circle and look forward to his continued awesomeness!"

–Kelly Lindstrom, senior relationship manager,
Allstate Affinity Solutions

"James possesses a visionary style of leadership balanced by strength and compassion. His development techniques deliver the right balance of support and independence, helping individuals to achieve even beyond their own expectations. He is driven, always focused on delivering meaningful results, while never forgetting the value of the resources under his watch. Additionally, his leadership and forward thinking have served him well in developing both effective strategic value coupled with well-crafted tactical execution. His demeanor during times of uncertainty and ambiguity has always displayed a strength of character and behavior that buoyed everyone through such events. James's background covers both the domestic as well as the global stage, making for a well-rounded resume of skills and experience. His time management, required to meet the demands of the business, has always been exemplary. His most notable leadership trait has always been his people agenda. He always makes time for anyone who needs it, offering sage advice and providing a framework of action upon which each individual could build to meet their personal objectives. His articulate and clear communication style exudes a strong sense of confidence, and well-thought-out ideas and conclusions. In summing up James' overall resume and skill set, I would state that there isn't any management or leadership training that I participated in that wasn't surpassed by my personal experiences in working with him!"

—Sam Costa, senior vice president, client delivery, Citigroup

"James is an exceptional leader with a resume full of notable accomplishments, talents, and skills that speak vividly for themselves. As someone who has been a colleague and friend to James for 14 years, I believe that what really sets him apart, however, is his character. James is crystal clear about his values and what matters most, and he "walks the talk" everyday in a way that inspires others and makes a unique and real difference in this world. James' dedication to being of service is exemplified in his book. What a gift to have the opportunity to learn firsthand from his story how to bring out the best in ourselves!"

—Randi Raskin Nash, executive coach and facilitator

Success on
Your Own Terms

6 Promises to Fire Up Your Passion, Ignite
Your Career, and Create an Amazing Life

• • • • • • • • • • • • • • • • •

By James B. Rosseau, Sr.

CAREER
PRESS
Pompton Plains, NJ

SUCCESS ON YOUR OWN TERMS
EDITED BY ROGER SHEETY
TYPESET BY DIANA GHAZZAWI
Cover design by Howard Grossman
Printed in the U.S.A.

To order this title, please call toll-free 1-800-CAREER-1 (NJ and Canada: 201-848-0310) to order using VISA or MasterCard, or for further information on books from Career Press.

CAREER
PRESS

The Career Press, Inc.
220 West Parkway, Unit 12
Pompton Plains, NJ 07444
www.careerpress.com

Library of Congress Cataloging-in-Publication Data
Rosseau, James B., 1971–
    Success on your own terms : 6 promises to fire up your passion, ignite your career, and create an amazing life / James Rosseau, Sr. ; foreword by Billy Dexter.
        pages cm
    Includes bibliographical references and index.
    ISBN 978-1-60163-315-6 (paperback) -- ISBN (invalid) 978-1-60163-471-9 (ebook)
    1. Career development. 2. Success. 3. Motivation (Psychology) I. Title.

HF5381.R77367 2014
650.1--dc23
                                                      2014008081

Acknowledgments

• •

First and foremost, I thank my Lord and Savior Jesus Christ, without whom none of this would be possible. I am certainly not deserving of the blessings and opportunities I've received, nor am I as smart as the accolades and accomplishments might make one believe. I am so grateful that I established a personal relationship with Jesus early in my life–that's not to say it's too late for anyone. But *truly* living is walking with HIM.

I would like to thank my wife of 17 years for being firm about our need to have Christ at the center of our relationship from the start, for being the best partner and help meet I could have through this journey, and for being a steady ear and comforter through the good times and the more challenging ones.

I want to thank my mother for showing me what hard work and sacrifice looks like. I didn't appreciate it then, but I "got it" years later. Thanks for working two or three jobs to help us maintain our life style, for taking the high road when Dad left, and for promoting and helping me maintain a relationship with him. Thank you for continuing to be strong in the face of numerous adversities.

I want to bless the memory of my father for briefly showing me what serving others looks like, whether as a pastor, a father (adopting several children), or an insurance agent.

I want to thank my son, James Jr. for his continuous, relentless pursuit of his passion (football), working through injury and adversity. His work passion and work ethic is an inspiration.

Lastly, I want to thank the countless mentors and co-journeymen that I have had the great fortune to learn from.

Contents

● ● ● ● ● ● ● ● ● ● ● ● ● ● ● ● ● ●

Foreword

● ●

Each person is born with a chance to create an amazing life full of opportunities and experiences that shape your beliefs, passions, and character. What is unique is that we all have been born into very different circumstances that shape our paths early on.

However, as each person reaches a crossroad at some point in his or her life, they have to make some key decisions. This period is unique to each individual.

Is this your time?

Success on Your Own Terms is a blueprint for how to prepare for these crossroads. We are at an amazing time in our country where the landscape is changing rapidly with technology, emerging global markets, social media, new civil liberties, and new careers that didn't exist five years ago. Are you prepared? *Success on Your Own Terms* is a playbook that helps you focus on your own passions and create a personal brand that lays the groundwork for a purposeful life and an amazing career.

As an executive search consultant and talent acquisitions expert for Fortune 500 companies, I talk to successful executives every day. One of the common denominators of very successful leaders is they have tapped into their passions and they all have a set of guiding principles that have led them through their personal and professional journeys.

James Rosseau does a masterful job of sharing his personal story of growing up in North Philadelphia and navigating the turbulent streets to follow his dreams in music and corporate America.

James didn't let setbacks detour him from his goals. He anticipated the setbacks and found ways to get around them. James discusses the power of education and the transformative lessons that help you to realize your dreams are possible. James has learned these lessons of fortitude and perseverance by having a personal strategy, hard work, and a commitment to help others.

As a teenager, I faced many obstacles getting out of the inner city of Detroit in the early '80s after high school. I had a close family, but none of my older three siblings or parents ever graduated from high school. I was searching for direction with no mentors or role models and no plan to guide me. What I did have, however, was a passion. My passion was that I wanted a different life than my family and I would do whatever it took to achieve it. Education was my outlet. I was not clear where that passion would lead me to, but I was crystal clear that I wanted it to take me someplace other than where I was. So my motivation and passion were around getting out of Detroit.

Success on Your Own Terms explores six promises that will help you build a foundation for a successful life and that will sustain you for a lifetime. The promises will help you tap into your passions and answer some questions: What gets you excited? What are you good at? What do you want out of your life?

As you begin to explore your passions, you start to develop a purpose and direction to build a life and a career platform. This platform helps you to create your personal brand and gives life meaning and direction.

I am so excited for you as you read *Success on Your Own Terms* because it will give you clarity on all aspects of your life but, more importantly, it will help you create a blueprint for your life and career. The lessons, examples, and stories that James shares with the readers are a true testament of his commitment to share with others so they can learn from his experiences.

It's your time now to have *Success on Your Own Terms*.

—Billy Dexter

1

Shift From Drift

• •

We've all heard the expression "Life is too short!" I would coun-ter that by saying, "Life is too long." What do I mean? Simply that life is too long *not* to be spending it doing something that you are genuinely passionate about.

This opening chapter creates the context and sets the stage for the essential six promises covered in this guide, all of which revolve around the promise to yourself to pursue your passion. Many of us are in a "crisis state"–wandering through the wilder-ness, often reactively, hoping that we find "success." This chapter compels us to make a paradigm shift, to view our life as a journey toward success on our own terms–the passion point.

At this very moment, according to the U.S. Department of Labor, there are 240 million people in the cycle of It. They are either:

- Getting ready for It.
- On the way to It.
- At It.
- Taking a break from It.
- On the way home from It.
- Decompressing from It.

What is the It? It is a job. In those jobs, few people take the initiative to innovate what they do and how they do it. People often say that you can't get to success by doing things your way. Few believe they can achieve success by creating custom-tailored life and business experiences based on their unique talents, interests, and dreams.

What will you do to achieve success your way?

Consider that you will spend decades in the workforce—and when I say decades, I am talking about roughly 7 million minutes of your life, when you calculate the average time spent working. It just doesn't make sense to invest all those years without connecting them to your dreams and talents. If you're going to spend that much time doing something, shouldn't it be something that stokes your inner fire, your passion, and allows you to innovate within your career and life?

Success is to be measured not so much by the position that one has reached in life as by the obstacles which he has overcome.
—*Booker T. Washington*

And yet, so few of us do! Recent survey results as reported in *Forbes* magazine indicate that only 20 percent of people are satisfied with their jobs. That means 80 percent are dissatisfied. That's a crippling statistic considering that every four out of five people are actively unhappy with what they are spending the days and years of their lives doing.

What gets in your way?

I appreciate that I have been extremely fortunate in my career, having made it to senior management roles as a member of an underrepresented group (black males), raised in urban Philadelphia, with a public school education, and without a college degree until my early 30s. Still, it wasn't at all a linear pathway. I too experienced "drift." On the surface, the circumstances of my life make my success look unlikely.

In my 20s, I realized that one of my passions was to show that there's another way out of the neighborhood besides drugs, music, sports, or in a coffin. As everyone comes up against obstacles, I will relate a few of mine and how I've marshaled the energies of passion, persistence, and a commitment to move through any impediment.

Passion sustains you

So why don't more people get jobs they enjoy? Is it because we are told from a young age what we *should* want, such as a great education or a high-paying job like a doctor, lawyer, or business executive? Does pursuing what we should want crowd out our passions?

One of the great things I enjoy watching in younger children is the pure view of life they bring to any activity. They still view, explore, imagine, believe, and act as if their dreams can come true. They don't think about boundaries, precedents, solvency, market opportunity, or the business case. They think about what they enjoy doing or believe they would enjoy doing, and then do it. Or they pretend to. Or, at least, they dream about doing it someday.

At some point, the realities of the world crowd in. Without meaning to, we, as a society, tend to steal those dreams away. These dreams often represent the passion that has already taken up residence in their hearts. You'll also find that these dreams are not just the common everyday desires, either. It isn't just the desire to be a rapper, actor, athlete, doctor, or lawyer. These uncommon dreams also include the inner city child who aspires to become an architect, the little girl who sees herself as a veterinarian, or the little boy who sees himself traveling on foreign mission trips.

One of the huge mistakes people make is that they try to force an interest on themselves. You don't choose your passions; your passions choose you.
—Jeff Bezos

Money comes and money goes, but having a passion can sustain you. Passion is like having access to an endless supply of fuel. Passion is what makes you fall seven times and stand up eight; it's what makes Olympic athletes train for four hard years, go to the Olympics, not make the medal stand, and then go right back into training for four more years for the opportunity to do it again.

How do I know this to be true? The simple answer is because passion has sustained me for most of my life. Following the principles found in this book, over a 25-year career, I've become president of a division of a Fortune 100 company. At the same time, no matter how successful I became in corporate life, I have continued my passionate pursuit of Christian hip-hop that combines all of my passions: music, innovation, and helping others. Later, you'll hear more about my story as "Trig," a Christian hip-hop artist turned producer, radio host, and media company owner. Fuel like that allows you to work a full day and a full night, and be ready for more the very next morning.

Dreams feed your passion

For as long as I can remember, I have enjoyed helping people achieve their dreams. Though I didn't necessarily think of it that way when I was younger, it was always there. Early in my business career, at a celebratory event, I was talking to our company CEO, Skip, my boss's boss. He asked me, "Why do you push and work so hard to do all of the things you are doing?" It was then that my second passion became crystal clear to me. My response was, "I want to be able to show people from the 'hood that you don't have to be a rapper, play basketball, or sell drugs to make it."

That revelation took us into a deeper conversation. Ultimately, I revealed to him that one day I wanted to go back into the old neighborhood driving a Lexus, showing them that I achieved success in a different way. But, more importantly, I wanted to show people that it was achievable for them as well. I wanted to help people see their way out of what they probably considered the destiny they were stuck with. And that is how I see this book as well.

Skip and I also discussed my first passion, music, and what I wanted to achieve in that particular realm. I told him about what I had been doing in the Christian hip-hop scene and how I wanted to bring together that community in an organized way.

In my 20s, I realized that my goal of becoming a CEO meant that I would be able to help even more people, which is not always the case in corporate America. In fact, when I finally get around to doing that PhD thesis, it's going to explore the myth that you have to be ruthless to be a CEO.

Athletic beginnings

I had a real desire to play football. It may have naturally grown out of the physical size that the Lord placed on me. Like many others, I worked to play Pop Warner football with the neighborhood team, the Nicetown Steelers. Dr. Hankerson, principal of Edward T. Steel Elementary School, which I attended, was the head coach.

In the summer of 1982, I was trying out for the 135-pound team. I wanted to make the team more than anything. I wanted to play fullback and had to compete against a good friend of mine for the spot. I wanted it so bad that, when I found I was over the weight limit, I went to great lengths to get my weight down. I would eat grapefruit three times a day and wear the infamous silver plastic suit several hours a day to sweat off some pounds. I made the team, albeit not starting at fullback, but playing tight end and defensive end.

In high school, I landed on the junior varsity team my first year and was working toward varsity for my sophomore year. During the Thanksgiving break, I was with a bunch of friends from the neighborhood, playing our regular Thanksgiving Day football game. The air was crisp. It was a little cold, of course, but we were having a great time. Although I didn't land a fullback spot on any official teams I was playing for, I still loved to run with the football. So naturally, during a kick-off, if the ball came my way, I took it.

During one such kick-off return, I ran toward the sideline, focusing only on "touchdown" in my head. Out of nowhere, a little boy stepped out onto the field and right into my path. There wasn't enough time to change course, so my only option was to try to hurdle over him. As I leapt, my back foot hit his head (he was okay, by the way). As a result, though, my left knee drove straight into the ground. I was in agonizing pain for a few minutes, but I thought that was it: just a few minutes of pain. Five minutes later, I was playing back in the game. But then, soon after, my knee gave out totally and I couldn't walk.

My friends helped me get home and, after hobbling around for a few days, I went to Temple Sports Medicine. As luck would have it, I had a crazy experience my first day there. I was sitting on a table in the back room waiting for a doctor. From my side I heard a voice say, "Tough break, kid." I looked up, and it was Andrew Tony, star point guard for the Philadelphia 76ers. Well, if anyone would know, he would. He'd had a bad string of injuries.

It turned out I had a torn ACL (anterior cruciate ligament) and, though I was able to have surgery, I received some interesting insights to go with it. The doctor told me that I was good to go from a normal, everyday mobility perspective, but to play football would be risky. If I took a significant hit, he cautioned, I could be re-injured and this time it could be worse, impairing my normal mobility off the field as well. That was it for my football career. I was crushed, to say the least. In hindsight, however, some years later, I came to a conclusion on this. As much as I loved it, football was neither my passion nor my purpose. I believe that if it truly had been, I would have taken the risk and played on.

Life, interrupted

My last year of high school was particularly difficult. I faced significant challenges with my father. After my parents split up, I lived with Dad for a time. Then he disappeared early in my senior year of high school. I dropped out of school, working full-time in an attempt to pay the bills and keep the home running. After realizing I couldn't sabotage my own future, I was able to get things right in school and turn failing grades into passing ones. In fact, I was recognized by Philadelphia's Channel 10 as the most improved student in the city at graduation.

During that year, it became clear to me that I wanted to be a communications major. Up until that time, I had focused a lot on music in various forms, whether playing instruments, rapping, or acting as a DJ, which certainly influenced my longer-term interests. As an English assignment, we were challenged to interview someone who was currently in the field we believed we wanted to be in. For me, it was radio, and I went to interview the one and only Doug Henderson, son of the legendary Jocko Henderson, at WDAS 105.3 FM in Philadelphia.

The interview was magical. Upon my arrival, Doug welcomed me into the studio and began telling me about how he got into the business. What was so cool about the interview is that he was also on air. So every now and then, as we were talking, he would say, "Excuse me a moment," spin his chair around to the microphone and jump on the air effortlessly with that deep, smooth voice. "This is Doug Henderson, playing those smooth grooves to get you home this afternoon. Hold your baby tight, and let her know it will be alllllll right," he would say. He was a pro!

That confirmed it for me. I left the DJ booth that day thinking, "I am going to go into radio," and as soon as I could, I applied for college as a communications major. I was ultimately accepted to Temple University. It was hard to believe. Between winning an award for the most improved student in the city from CBS Channel 10 news (and the money that came with it), looking forward to a great summer ahead, and now acceptance to Temple, things were on a roll.

The first morning at Temple felt surreal. I arrived ready to get my books and my roster, and get going. I was ready to start my classes. Of course, there were all of the prerequisite courses, orientation, overviews of the fraternities you can join, the rules and regulations, how to support the school's sports teams, and what seemed like a never-ending list of things to do. I just wanted to get to the communications classes—please! "Fine," I said to myself, "I'll do what it takes to get there." By the middle of the afternoon, I was called down to the administrative offices. On arrival, I was abruptly notified that my financial aid had fallen through. My initial reaction was, "Okay, so what do we do now?" I was informed that I had to fix that issue: no payment, no school.

Upon further investigation, it was clear. My mother didn't make enough to qualify for the various loans, but made too much for us to get grants. As far as we knew, there were no alternatives. So there I was, crushed yet again. First I'd lost my hopes of playing pro football courtesy of a knee injury, and now, because of some paperwork and perceived financial problems, I couldn't go to college.

I couldn't believe that this was being taken from me, particularly after I had gotten over the football setback a few years before and had re-focused my energy.

I'll admit it: I was mad at God for real.

Death comes calling

I believe that every young boy wants the attention, approval, and perhaps even the admiration of his father. It is hard for us to admit that as men. We often form the belief that we cannot show our emotional needs because it's not "manly." However, these emotional needs are very real. With more young men than ever growing up without a father in the home or in their lives, there is a significant gap relative to the emotional connection needed with a father to help a young man develop.

Absent filling that gap, I believe that many men walk the days of their lives seeking attention, approval, and admiration from others. As a result, men seek to consciously or subconsciously do the things they believe will secure that same attention. Though I was fortunate to have my father in my life during my early years, as a child I never felt like I measured up to his expectations. Unfortunately, he passed away before I was ever able to prove I did. Although he never said it out loud, I felt like what I did was never good enough. If I scored a 95 on a test, for example, I felt like I needed it to be 100 to get his approval. Though I can't point to examples of him saying he wasn't satisfied, I also can't find ones of him celebrating successes with me or, if he did, I don't remember them.

My father was an insurance agent by trade, as well as a pastor of a small church, Triumph the Church and the Kingdom of God in Christ. It had a long name, but it was a small church in West Philadelphia. Every Sunday had the same routine: up early, get ready, grits and fish for breakfast, then off to church—or at least trying to go to church, as Mom often ran a little late. Dad and I sat in the car waiting, as he grumbled, "Come on, Gail. I'm the pastor. I can't be late for church."

That small church in West Philadelphia, with no more than 10 benches on each side, was like a second home. Mom often conducted service, and Dad waited in the pulpit, ready to preach. I usually stayed in the back of the church, having fun with my friends, Stacy and Freddie. Often, we got caught not paying attention, and then came the evil eye from Mom up front. After church, we often went to either one of two places for lunch: Ida's or the Divine Lorraine Hotel on Broad Street, both in the North Philadelphia area. We ate heartily, went home, somehow getting into a pillow fight and then, as I remember, it was time to take an afternoon nap. I hated the last part; I just wanted to go outside and play with my friends, but Dad always made us take an afternoon nap.

My mother and father also adopted several children along the way in my younger years. Ivan Bonner stayed with us for quite a while. We used to call ourselves "7-11" (mocking the name of the well-known chain stores in Philly), as I was "7" and Ivan was "11." I learned a lot from him during the years we grew up together. Ivan treated me like a younger brother and showed me the ropes on many things, like how to attract young ladies, shaving, bathing more regularly, and dressing more attractively. We got in trouble together and, once, almost got thrown out of the house together by my mother. She gave us trash bags to pack our clothes and everything, but I knew she wasn't going to throw us out. (Okay, I'll admit it. I was really scared.)

In retrospect, what I've taken away from all of these experiences, observing my father in everything he did, was that I learned he had a clear passion for people. Pastoring is about helping people; working as an insurance professional is about helping people prepare for their needs and aiding them as they pick up the pieces after an unfortunate event. Adopting children is about helping a young person have a home with love and alternatives.

This was our family's life for a while. Although I wasn't directly getting some of the things I needed as a young man, I think the family structure and its consistency, along with our time at the church, helped fill the perceived gap. Unfortunately, my father and mother got divorced when I was in my early teens. The night my father left felt tragic. He and my mother argued as he was leaving the house. A man I then called "Uncle Tom" pulled him away, saying, "Come on, James. We should go." Years later, I got a much better understanding about some of the events surrounding that night.

As time passed, missing my father, I decided to move in with him and my grandmother. Why did I do such a thing, when I felt like he didn't celebrate me enough as a person? Well, because, like most young men, I was still in pursuit of his attention and approval. When I initially moved in, it felt great. I had a large bedroom all to myself. My father even let me use the basement for my passion of music. I turned the basement into a nice studio of sorts with my DJ equipment and keyboard. And there was enough room for practice space with my group. However, between us, nothing had really changed. In fact, things got much worse.

I was 16 or 17, driving my own car, and working an after-school job, and I had a girlfriend. Times were good. One day, I got some great news at school. I picked up Tracy, my girlfriend at the time, and rushed home to tell my father. I couldn't wait. Whatever the news, I felt it was important enough to get to Dad right away. I ran up the steps, turned the corner, and barged into his room. To my devastation he was in bed with "Uncle Tom" and "Uncle Bob." Damn!

My heart sank as I turned and walked out, or *ran* out. I jumped into the car and drove for a while, finally stopping and sitting in a field of grass over by the eye hospital near Broad Street. I felt totally betrayed, asking myself over and over, "How could my father be gay? How could he be in that type of a relationship with Uncle Tom and Uncle Bob? Wait, how long has this been going on? Wait, is this why he and Mom are divorced?"

As the months marched on, things continued to deteriorate. Sure, we talked. He apologized for letting me find out that way. He told me he loved me, but there was more to it. Not long after, I found out that my father also had a drug problem, and suddenly it all started to make sense. I had been trying to figure out why things were changing. I mean, the divorce was one thing, but no more pastoring (or church for that matter); the insurance job went away; and he was now driving a cab. Once all the pieces came together, there it was.

One day, during the early part of my senior year in high school, Dad didn't come home. The next day came and went, and no Dad. Days passed until the end of the week, and still no Dad. I was distraught to say the least. There I was, just Grandma and me, and I didn't know what to do. Grandma was elderly and not working, and we still had bills to pay.

I went to the owner of the store where I worked after school and asked for more hours, and he was nice enough to give them to me. I left school early or just cut all day sometimes to get the hours in, hoping to pay the bills—a farfetched idea. I only realized too late that I could not earn nearly enough to keep up with the bills.

After a time, I raised the white flag and called my mother. She was all too happy to help. In fact, she was so eager for me to get my life back on track that my grandmother and I moved in with my mother.

Years passed and no word from Dad. Then one day I found out that he was staying at a halfway house in North Philly. I went to investigate. Sure enough, he was there. He looked rough, but I didn't care. I was glad to know he was alive. For all I knew, he could have been dead all those years.

I was full of mixed emotions: happy to find him alive, but angry, sad, and confused that he never reached out to establish contact after leaving home. He was clearly recovering from drug usage, but had come a long way. He had recovered enough so that the owner of the halfway house had made him a supervisor and, I believe, had provided him with a furnished apartment across the street.

Upon going to his apartment, I found that he was lacking a lot of things. As Temple University hadn't worked out and I didn't have funds for college, I decided to work and try to save up some money, so I took on several jobs. I worked at a parking lot from mid-afternoon to early evening. I had a day job serving yogurt and making salads at Everything Yogurt in Liberty Place on Chestnut Street. I also had an overnight valet and doorman position at the Four Seasons Hotel on Benjamin Franklin Parkway. I was making pretty good tips and had the luxury of coming across lost articles in the hotel, so I was able to help Dad with some men's clothing, a few dollars for groceries, and whatever he needed.

It felt so strange helping out my own father. Then again, that's what he had taught me growing up. His whole life had been about helping others until he could no longer help himself. I was visiting Dad regularly. For me, it was like a wound finally starting to heal. It wasn't perfect, by any measure, but what relationship is? What was important was the time we were spending together, time to talk and, hopefully, reconcile with one another. And, who knows, perhaps get his attention, approval, and admiration after all.

One day, I came by to visit him but there was no answer at his door. I knocked several times, waited patiently, but still no answer. I then went over to the halfway house to ask a few people I had come to know during my visits. But no one had seen him. I returned again a few days later, same thing; a week later, same thing; two weeks later and still no luck. Once again, Dad had disappeared. Angry, sad, and confused, I didn't know what to do. The one upside was that I felt a bit more optimistic that he was alive now—having gone through what I would call this first cycle with him.

About a year passed from the time of my father's second disappearance. One day I received a letter notifying me that my dad was in Harlem, New York. "What the heck is he doing up in Harlem?" I thought. By this time, my son, James Jr., was born, so I took him on a trip to Harlem to meet his grandfather. When I arrived at the address, I found that it was a YMCA. Dad was living in a tiny room with just a bed and a hot plate. It was very sad, but again, this was Dad. I was happy to see him, but our reunion was short-lived. The next time I came to see him, he was gone again.

When I next found my father, I saw a rapid decline in his health. Then one day, I got word that he had passed away. I was at my mother's house, stopping by for a visit. My brother, Brenton, who was very young at the time, said, "Your dad died." I was at a loss. I knew that it was a long shot, but I had still hoped that my father and I would be able to spend time together, that he would have a chance to see me do well and get to

Take advantage of every opportunity; where there is none, make it for yourself.
—Marcus Garvey

know his grandson. The three of us were going to do things and, for lack of a better term, get some "Huxtable" time in. It was hard to move from "improbable" to "clearly not going to happen."

My whole life became a whirlwind after that. My mother was great in helping put together the funeral and all of the other arrangements. We did everything in Philadelphia, and despite Dad's long absence from his church, there was still a good turnout. I was pretty strong through it all, but I think I was just overwhelmed and performing on autopilot. There was a lot going on, and I was still in disbelief and tremendously saddened. I completely lost it when they tried to close the casket. I literally stopped them from closing it. I wasn't ready to say goodbye at that point: goodbye to my father; goodbye to the possibility of securing his approval and admiration; goodbye to the possibility of learning from his example.

For years after that, I kept things bottled up. I certainly worked hard at everything I did, perhaps harder than before, but I believe I lost some balance along the way. After a lifetime without my father's attention, where was I going to get it now? I didn't have any other male role models at the time, nor did I seek them out. Instead, through the years, I let these scars evolve.

If I can do it, so can you

"How can I best share the things I have learned through the years?" I asked myself this question, as the possibility of a book percolated in my mind. Today's conventional wisdom would say my background and life experiences are not the "usual suspects" for career or life success. However, that is exactly one of the reasons I wrote this book.

During the last few years, there has been a noticeable increase in the subject of how to advance your career. This question leaves many people searching for the proverbial secrets of success. As I continued to think about the topic and what I could share that might be meaningful, I ultimately decided that I wanted to focus on things that I believed were key life lessons along my journey.

After working for 25 years, and through trial and error, I finally realized something powerful. I understood and acknowledged that it wasn't a random set of acts or events that produced the success and joy I have felt in my career. Actually, the success I've created has grown out of a repeatable set of acts—a model—if you will. The model is simple to use and is made up of six tenets or promises. Within this book I will share that model through my personal journey and a select set of stories that are intended to empower you.

Knowing what I know now, I want to help others avoid what I consider a crisis state. The truth is, if you don't know what you're chasing, you *are* in a crisis state. What if, based on my stories and experiences, you could avoid the downward spiral? What if the continuum, starting with disappointment and disenchantment, leading ultimately to failure, could be completely reversed with success as the result?

How to shift from drift

What I learned in going through the challenges, in encountering roadblocks and obstacles, is that I have to be true to myself. These six promises are commitments that I've made to myself and mindfully put into practice in every situation that I've been in. My advice, from someone who has been there, is to make these six promises and keep them:

1. **Embrace your passion.** Don't discount your dreams. Return to that childlike fascination you once had and find a way to spend your work and life passionately!

2. **Perform to progress versus perfection.** Most of us have experienced the paralysis that often comes from perfection or the pursuit of it. Here is an alternative to the paralysis of perfection: what if you performed to progress toward your goals and dreams, celebrating each small step along the way? As I referenced before, passion is at the root of the promises. It is a key part of

the larger process of fueling your progress. However, the world doesn't reward dreamers for dreaming, but for doing. You must also perform at the highest possible level, seeking progress with each new skill set learned and action taken.

3. **Promote with purpose.** Let people know who you are in a way that is personal and purposeful. No one enjoys the slick self-promoter. People will, instead, recognize and reward those who stand confidently in their strengths authentically and purposefully.

4. **Parlay your platform.** Your "platform" is the station in life you've achieved thus far. It may not be where you want to be yet, but it is yours! It includes your network of friends, coworkers, your mentors, and even those bosses who partner with you to achieve your passions, just as you've helped them achieve theirs. Your platform is the sum total of all your efforts in honing your talents and skills. It's that sense of confidence and awareness you've grown into and developed by walking the path of your life, including insights gleaned from all your business experiences.

5. **Put it into action.** I don't believe that opportunity knocks only once. I believe it knocks often. But we have to keep our eyes and ears open to see and hear it when it does! Often, opportunity stares us in the face and we're too busy working to notice. Instead, be alert and aware. Take action on the four steps that lead up to this one as earnestly and as often as possible.

6. **Practice philanthropy.** Give. You can never go wrong giving, even when nobody hears about it. Giving helps not just those to whom you give but also helps you find the purpose to give and give again. So many of us have benefited from the gifts of others, and you'll never know what your small, or even not-so-small, gift might mean

to someone in need, be it a coworker, a friend, or even a boss. As you find success, make giving a habit commensurate with your earnings.

First and foremost, you are making these promises to yourself within the context of being the very best *you* possible. I am a strong believer in my Christian faith, and believe that we are all designed and called to fulfill a purpose. Not everyone is going to applaud you along the way as you fulfill that purpose. You have to create the expectation of success so that you have motivation to draw from as you move forward.

Find comfort in committing to and fulfilling the promises you make to yourself. Others can't run the race for you. You can only run it for yourself. If that means turning around at the "Finish" line and being the only one there to pat your back, then go on and pat it! I encourage you to begin reading this book, and committing to making and keeping these six promises to yourself. I firmly believe that these tenets are universally applicable, regardless of your vocation, interests, or background. These promises are practical and easy to remember, and will prevent you from going into a crisis state. These are six proven ways to innovate your career.

You have a monumental choice before you: how you will invest your time, energy, and, ultimately, your life. This is not about your education level or formal training. This is about your willingness to take action on these six promises and to make them a part of your daily routine. Remember, it is not always the large, Hollywood ending or the "Rocky" moments that determine our success. Instead, it's the small things we do daily, habitually, that make us successful. Based on my life experiences, I have created the game plan and road map I wish I had when I started out. I share it with you now. Let's get started!

> *The lack of expectation of success takes away a powerful incentive to succeed.*
> —George Subira

2

Promise 1: Embrace the Passion

• •

Maybe it's tempting to play small, to go for the safe path, to settle and take the well-traveled road in front of us. Ask yourself how long you can continue on that road without the jet-fuel that passion provides. Then consider Nelson Mandela's observation: "There is no passion to be found playing small—in settling for a life that is less than the one you are capable of living." In this life, passion blows the doors open. Yes, going after what you really want, what you're really passionate about, demands so much—time, effort, sacrifice, and even pain along the way. Though playing small might seem easier in some ways, it also comes with nagging thoughts.

They tug at your sleeve asking, "Is this all there is? Is this the best I can do?" It is while on the path of pursuing your passions and following your dreams that you truly come alive. This is where you experience heart-soaring triumphs and soul-moving times that shape and mold you. As the saying goes, the problem is never that you aim too high and miss the mark. The real problem is aiming too low and hitting the mark. When you choose to settle for less, you almost always miss out on the generosity and energy that life has in store for you.

Every now and then, I get together with some of the friends from my youth. No matter how much time passes between visits, when we see each other again it's just like the good old days. What I've observed through the years is how much we have all changed during the process of growing up. For those of us with clear passions or goals, who chose to embrace that approach, our passions led us down diverse paths and helped us progress. We advanced on many different fronts: family, career, and community involvement, to name just three.

Unfortunately, a few of my friends, for whatever reason, did not lock into their passion. They either aimed too low, such as focusing on just having a good job, or they didn't aim at all. As time passes, I see a world of difference between the two groups—those who embraced their passions and those who did not. The ones who have taken their passions to heart always seem to have a lot of energy, their lives buzzing with excitement. They can't help but talk about their activities with enthusiasm, often sharing something related to their journey. The other group, those who did not pursue their passions, seldom expresses any sense of excitement. In fact, it often seems like they just exist and are simply going through the motions.

A few months ago during a discussion with a friend of mine, something really stuck with me. During our chat, I asked about what he was doing in his life: what was he working on, who was he spending time with, what was he looking forward to, and what was he excited about? He struggled to answer these questions. Most of his responses were a series of mumbled words or a simple "I don't know." He then said, "I don't know if I have a purpose in my life," and that saddened me. I could see the lifelessness in his eyes. I almost felt guilty. I had just updated him on my progress with this book, my new job, Holy Culture, Corelink Radio, and a number of other things. Now, having shared the things I was so excited about, things that were in line with my passions for music, innovation, and helping others, I felt sad to see his emptiness. He left feeling sad, and I was left with the conviction that I needed to finish this book. Once it's out there, it can be a source for helping people find or re-engage with their passions and be a tool to help them with their journeys.

Your passion point

I want to encourage you, at whatever stage of life you're currently in, to become a kid again—because this is where your dreams began. Close your eyes and think back to when you were 10, 11, or 12 years old. What was it that you wanted to do with your life? What did you know in your heart that you would do? Similar to the process of hypnosis, I invite you to relive those uninhibited years where you actively dreamed and truly believed you could be anything you wanted to be and do whatever you dreamed about. Together, let's take a step forward and embrace those dreams with eyes wide open, accepting them as your passion point.

What is a passion point? I believe that we're all born with abilities and desires. There's an internal blueprint. Your task is to bring it to the surface. These things we are passionate about, our passion points, emerge into the world in our own unique way and combinations. I know when I was growing up that I loved music and creating new things, and was passionate about leading people. But I didn't know how those passions would play out in my life.

We create our life by pursuing interests that drive us and by our reaction to the events that happen to us—both of which we get to choose. We're all born with immense, natural talents. As children we gladly try them on, opening our hearts and minds to the seemingly limitless possibilities the world has to offer. But they slip away from us as we get older. *If we create our life,*

I was blessed with certain gifts and talents, and God gave them to me to be the best person I can be and to have a positive impact on other people.
—Bryan Clay

we can re-create it, too. You owe it to yourself to look deep inside. Look at what drives you, what you feel passionate about. You may feel that you don't have any special talents or particular passions, but I believe you just haven't found them yet.

I want to help you tap into and develop those talents and show you where to look for inspiration. I share my stories to show you that embracing your passion comes in many different forms. Inspiration is as close as the people in your life right this minute. I encourage you to read the stories of my personal experiences and apply them to your life. Piggyback your dreams on what I've learned and shared from these encounters. You too can pursue your childhood passions. I encourage you to dream big!

Doing well by doing good

When I was in my 20s, I decided that I wanted to become a CEO one day. I knew I wanted to help others, and that seemed like the most powerful position you could be in to effect change. I believe that when you help others pursue their dreams, you help the immediate ecosystem and, in a grander way, society. We have all seen the movies, the news stories, and articles about the ruthless CEO. The common portrayal is that in order to be a successful CEO, you need to be heartless. I believe that is a myth that most of us buy into: that you can't do well by doing good. When I complete my doctorate in the future, I plan to write my thesis (or antithesis, actually!) on *doing well by doing good.* So many people get caught up in believing that you can't do good things for others and still do well for yourself. This is akin to the "nice guy finishes last" syndrome. From my experience, that is simply not true. You can indeed help others and prosper as a result.

Invest in people

I've admired many people over the course of my life, many of whom have invested in me. They have given their time, talents, energy, and efforts that tapped into passions already present in my life, or they sparked passions I didn't realize I had. It all began when I was 14 and had the good fortune of working for a man named Joe Jankowski. Joe owned a nearby hardware store called Nicetown Lock and Hardware.

In some ways, I really didn't want that summer job. I was like every kid, wanting to play all summer–basketball, football, you name it. However, I also had a burning passion to be a DJ and knew this summer job could help me earn the money for turntables. Up until that point, I'd borrowed turntables to fuel this DJ passion. Given my mother's advice about my need to support my own habits, I knew she wasn't going to purchase them. I was going to the neighborhood Boys and Girls Club on a regular basis. They had a summer work program where they partnered with several local businesses to bring in kids to work during summer vacation for a modest wage. My friend Farrell and I went to work for Joe at Nicetown Lock and Hardware. The store was located right around the corner from my house, so it was very convenient.

Initially, I was not thrilled about the idea of working at a hardware store, as I envisioned myself making keys and doing other boring tasks all day. However, I was focused on getting my turn-tables, so I proceeded full steam ahead.

When I first started, I met Joe and the store manager, Chuck. They were both great people. They knew a lot about the hardware store business and were very willing to share, particularly Joe. First he taught me how to make keys. Then he taught me how to install new glass in windows and doors. Joe taught me how to do light electrical and plumbing work, then introduced me to the Security Plus company he owned with a partner, John. They installed alarm systems and provided maintenance. He showed me how to do some of that work as well. Throughout it all, Joe was patient and instructive. I watched whenever a customer came into the store with something broken. I would be ready to say, "We don't do that," and Joe would say, "Let me take a look at it." If someone needed help fixing something, the scope of the project didn't matter. Joe always looked at it to see if he could help.

After spending time with Joe during that summer, it was clear to me that if something could be fixed, he either knew how to do it or would figure out how to do it. He had a knack for it, or dare I say, a passion.

If a leader doesn't convey passion and intensity then there will be no passion and intensity within the organization, and they'll start to fall down and get depressed.

—Colin Powell

Before I knew it, the summer was over and the mission was, well, half accomplished. I had enough money saved to buy one turntable. They were about $400 each. However, more than that—and I didn't realize it at the time—I had gained a whole new set of skills, from sales, to fixing things, to doing inventory, and much more. My exposure to various situations and Joe's mentoring were invaluable.

As the summer ended, Joe asked me if I was interested in working after school. In a heartbeat, I decided to continue. As you can imagine, our relationship grew through the years, and so did my appreciation for Joe. When I turned 16 and purchased my first car, it was a dinged-up, 1970 Volkswagen Beetle. It was missing the back window, had a fender or two loose and hanging off, a weak floor in the backseat, and too many other things wrong to remember. Who wanted to help work on it? You guessed it: Joe. He and a buddy helped me fix the fenders and do some work to make the old thing look better. Over the next year, Joe gave me keys to the store and allowed me to close it by myself during the week and then open it on Saturdays.

I've recalled Joe in my memories countless times through the years. He didn't make a ton of money, he wasn't famous or extremely popular, but he had a clear passion: fixing things and helping people. He got a lot of joy sharing his knowledge and experience with me. Joe is someone I look back on and think about fondly every time something good happens to me. I've wanted to call Joe many times and tell him all about my successes and wins as they've happened. Sadly, I lost track of Joe. I still think about him as the person who first inspired my interest in doing well by doing good.

Build a network

About three years later, after the hardware store and doing some odd jobs, I began to think about having a job with more stability, with benefits, and so forth. I applied for and landed a job at Today's Man as a security guard. It wasn't very exciting work, but it was a good company (a bit more professional than the other jobs I had worked thus far), with decent pay and good benefits. One day, the vice president of stores, Don Fleming, was visiting. As he stood at the front of the store near my security stand, I struck up a conversation with him. I told him that I was going to the Computer Learning Center at night in order to become a computer programmer (following my innovation passion). Don then asked me to walk him around the store to give him an overview of how I did things. It gave us time to have a conversation. I shared some of my aspirations with him. Toward the end of our discussion, Don turned to me and said, "You know, instead of working security, I think we should try to get you an opportunity at corporate head-quarters." I was shocked. And so were the store managers, as it all happened quickly.

Within a few weeks, Don helped me secure a role in the ac-counting department at the Today's Man headquarters in New Jersey. I started there as a credit card data entry person. I was a good typist and I did well at the job. This was my first experi-ence in a corporate environment, allowing me to meet people in various departments, including human resources, receiving, pur-chasing, and marketing. Also, because it was headquarters, I often saw the CEO, CFO, and other functional heads, providing me the opportunity to get to know many of them. I made sure I stayed in touch with Don from time to time, as I considered him a mentor of sorts. As he obviously played a key role in getting me to corpo-rate, I wanted to keep him abreast of my progress. I never asked Don why he helped me, but I do recall him mentioning something about my assertiveness in chasing after my goals. He liked that about me and noticed it even during our brief conversation. It mo-tivated him to help.

At Today's Man, my supervisor, Allison, became pregnant and was preparing to head out to maternity leave. During that time, I did everything I could to position myself as someone who could do her job during her leave. My supervisor reported to Barry Pine, who was the assistant controller. Barry was also someone with whom I'd been able to secure a good working relationship. When Allison departed for maternity leave, Barry offered me the super-visory role, which I gladly accepted. Over time, I asked Barry to learn about additional jobs in the department. He provided me with opportunities to assist in accounts payable, accounts receiv-able, and other areas fulfilling a variety of functions.

Barry eventually offered me a role in running payroll. Even though I had no idea what it entailed, I immediately said yes and took the risk. The fact that Barry offered me an additional opportunity made me realize that my focused, proactive efforts were bearing fruit. It also revealed Barry's confidence in my continued progression within the organization. However, that also meant I needed to make good on Barry's investment. I took every book home that I could about how Today's Man's process payroll, the process within the stores to collect the time the employees were working, the time clock system, the core payroll system, how checks were distributed, how we executed direct deposit—you name it. If it was written down someplace, I read it, as I wanted to be as prepared as possible.

In this new position, I connected with people from every department, including the HR team, distribution, purchasing, marketing, and the management at every store across the country. This is where I really began to establish my network.

I found that I was enjoying the work and decided to pursue further involvement within the profession. I became a member of the American Payroll Association, as well as joining the local regional payroll users' group. The users' group was an excellent opportunity, as it allowed people within the profession to get together on a regular basis, share the best practices, and learn from each other. These experiences also broadened my network, as they gave me the opportunity to establish working relationships with others in the same profession at different organizations. The group was headed by Brenda Snipes, who was the user president of the group. Brenda and I quickly formed a great working relationship and, before I knew it, I assumed a leadership role within the users' group and succeeded Brenda as president several years later.

Throughout all of this, I stayed in contact with Don and Barry, as both had been instrumental in my progression within the organization. Each man had seen abilities in me, and had sparked my interest in and commitment to learning as much as I could. They often offered me the opportunity to work at new store openings, assisting with the set-up of the security system, as well as training management on payroll procedures.

After almost three years at Today's Man, I was called about an opportunity to work at Wilmington Savings Fund Society (WSFS) in Wilmington, Delaware. The job opportunity was broader in scope, providing me a chance to learn a host of new things with a compensation package to match. I believe the headhunter who called me about the WSFS position learned about me via my activities and involvement within the regional payroll users' group. My experience, even this early in my career, further underscores the importance of networking.

Focus on making an impact

I was really looking forward to this new and exciting opportunity, particularly as the pay raise provided me with enough money to get my first apartment—very important! The job was located in downtown Wilmington, Delaware, and the role was payroll/human resources information systems manager. My responsibilities centered on ensuring employee payment and maintaining employee records.

During my first week on the job, I was faced with a situation that I had never experienced before. Apparently the IRS had done some auditing. They found the organization owed some payroll taxes and literally stopped in to collect the taxes! You have to understand that, typically, the IRS sends a letter. You have the chance to respond and then settle everything through the mail or by phone. I was shocked to get a call one day from the assistant controller that "a representative from the IRS is here to see you." My first thought was, "See me? I just got here!"

I headed to the conference room to meet with the assistant controller and the gentleman from the IRS. I was almost speechless when he told me the IRS's position: "You are behind in your payroll taxes. You're a bank. Write us a check, now!" Fortunately, I was able to explain that I was new to the organization and needed some time to review, get caught up to speed on the situation, and then propose a resolution.

It was during this time that I discovered that the organization had recently invested in a great HR management system. However, the employee records had not been entered into the system. That meant I had a project to undertake. Over the next several weeks, I worked feverishly to establish order within the group by setting clear goals and focusing on fundamentals. In order to do this, I spent time talking with my manager, Susan Highfield, as well as colleagues and other people from key areas within the organization in order to gain their perspectives. This allowed me to synthesize key themes and develop my goals.

Several items were common across each of my conversations: improving the payroll accuracy rate (essentially meaning that we pay people correctly the first time); creating a data model within the HR management system to ensure record consistency; financial reporting for senior management as well as for regulatory needs; and last, but certainly not least, improving the process for posting the payroll to the general ledger, as our lack of accuracy or timeliness impacted the financial records of the company.

This approach was hard for me, discipline wise, because I saw so many opportunities and I naturally tend to multi-task. However, what I learned here is how important it is to focus on a few key areas that can make the biggest impact. By doing this, I was able to concentrate and achieve more in less time. I had often heard of the 80/20 rule. This rule states that 20 percent of what you do will yield 80 percent of your results. This experience gave me the hands-on opportunity to see this rule in action. Putting it to work for our team, we successfully accomplished major improvements in a short period of time.

Drive on

In chapter 1, I mentioned my father's passing, but the story and its impact on my life warrant me walking through it in a little more detail. One day, I received a letter from a nun in New York City. In the letter she informed me that she knew of my father's location and that she had been trying to reach me for some time. Later in the week, I went to visit my father; he was now a patient in a hospital in Harlem. Though I certainly wanted to take my son and wife, I decided to go by myself for the first visit as I wasn't sure what to expect.

Love the life you live.
Live the life you love.
—*Bob Marley*

I was nervous when I arrived at the hospital. When I stepped off the elevator onto his floor, something felt really strange. I had been to hospitals before, but this felt different. As I walked down the hallway, I couldn't help but notice how much plastic dominated the area and that gloves were hanging outside the doors of each of the rooms. When I got to his room, I paused before entering, noticing that everyone who entered the room, visitors and doctors alike, were required to wear gloves. It turns out that Dad was now HIV positive and not doing well at all. He was deteriorating, both mentally and physically.

It was difficult to see him, much less talk to him, in that condition. I could tell he was in pain: his eyes winced, his mouth trembled, and his body movements were erratic. Prior to this, my father was a fairly large man; well over 6 feet tall, with a strong body frame. But this condition had dramatically reduced his size.

It was hard to talk given his condition, but it didn't matter; every distraction and barrier that might have existed prior to that moment began to disappear. I found that I was like any other child, just happy to be speaking with my father! He told me he was tired of the hospital food and that he wanted some real food—some soul food. I quickly made tracks and found him some, and stayed with him to help him enjoy it.

I left that day planning to visit him again within the next week. Unfortunately, he passed away before I had a chance to visit again. His passing was devastating for me, as it definitely took away what I was hoping to achieve in our relationship. During my childhood, I never really felt like I had his approval, something I was hoping to shift over time. Now that possibility was gone. It certainly was not an easy time for me, but I needed to drive on.

Seek out mentors

I returned to work and gained some comfort with the progress I had made to date. I even decided to try my hand at some other things. My desire to lead others was growing. As I was already active with the regional payroll users' group, I decided to become a board member. From there, I eventually became president of the group. This placed me in a very influential role, allowing me to work more closely with the leadership at Ceridian, the payroll processing organization that the members of the users' group used. This led to a number of speaking opportunities and contributions to published articles on industry topics and best practices.

Internally, I continued that habit I'd developed with Barry at Today's Man, asking my manager (now Vicky Myoda) for additional opportunities for development. Vicki was very supportive. Over time, I took on responsibilities for employee relations and compensation matters. From there I became the HR manager, which gave me access to the CEO of the organization, Marvin Schoenhals (Skip).

During a celebration gathering for completing a project, I had the opportunity to chat with Skip. Up until then, all of our conversations had been transactional, dealing with in-the-moment HR issues and planning. However, that celebration gave us some time to just talk. At one point during the conversation, he asked me, "What inspires you to work so hard?" I didn't know how to answer the question initially as it caught me off guard. But I recalled that Skip mentioned to me that he was surprised that someone as young as I was had such an important role in our company.

My response was simple: "Skip, I don't see many people from my neighborhood make it big. I want to be able to go back to the neighborhood one day driving a Lexus and not only show what I had attained, but how they could do it as well." My point was that I wanted to prove that inner city youth, in particular African-American males, were not limited to the stereotypes of success that we are often associated with. In other words, I don't have to be an athlete, rapper, or drug dealer to have a nice home, car, or lifestyle.

> *It is your passion that empowers you to be able to do that thing you were created to do.*
> —T. D. Jakes

That conversation sparked a relationship between Skip and me, and from there he became a mentor. He made himself available and coached me through a number of key things I was trying to accomplish. I had a business idea that I wanted to bring to fruition. Skip participated as I worked on a business plan, reviewing the plan with me on several occasions. He even assisted in meeting with some venture capitalists to get an objective view. All of this provided me with invaluable insight early in my career.

My great business venture at that time was to begin a record label. Inside, the dreams that began with a 14-year-old boy who got his first job in order to buy a turntable had not died. The passion I felt in actively pursuing music had never gone away. As I got older, my view of that business changed significantly, and so I put it on hold.

After a few years and a number of crucial learning experiences at WSFS, I began to seek out a new career opportunity. By establishing strong working relationships that often extended into mentoring relationships, I had a considerable base of resources to assist me in framing potential opportunities.

The management team at WSFS worked with me to consider a number of opportunities within the bank, including the branch system. I visited a few branches to "live a day in the life" and experience things first hand. I discovered that this did not pique my interest, but I was very appreciative of the experience, as it removed that question mark from my list of possibilities. I was eventually contacted by a recruiter about a great opportunity at NovaCare and, before long, made the move. I was off to the next leg of my journey!

Tap into your passion

Each of these experiences and relationships I cultivated through the years helped to foster different aspects of myself. The individuals I worked alongside and learned from, led by example, proving to me that you can do well by doing good. By taking the time to mentor me, they helped me to get a better start in my career. Little did I know that working in a hardware store as a teenager would help develop my lifelong love and pursuit of music. Or that striking up a conversation with the vice president of stores while I was on duty as a security guard would set me on the path to leadership. As a Christian, I know that these people did not come into my life by happenstance; there was a reason we connected. These people helped me turn my passions into doable and attainable goals. By being inquisitive and open to cultivating new relationships, I was able to put the pieces of the puzzle together. When a mentor sparked an interest of mine, I regularly asked myself questions. I tried to figure out the answers like where I could take that interest and how I could develop to the next level.

So how do you embrace your passion in life? How do you tap into those dreams and turn them into reality? You can start by keeping an open mind when you walk into different situations and meet new people. Be interested and develop a natural curiosity about the world around you. You will find that, as you listen to the stories that others share, parts of them will resonate within you, helping you tap into your own passions. Dig deep to figure out what drives you or lights a fire within you!

How do you find the wonderful people who will make a difference in your life? Be tuned in to the people

Man is only great when he acts from passion.
—Benjamin Disraeli

around you and seek out those who interest you. If you don't have someone in mind, ask around and see if someone else knows a person who would be a great fit for you. Make requests for people to be your mentors. I know this may not come naturally to everyone, but if you practice and learn how to make good requests, mentors will appear. It may be your boss or an influential person whom you trust and respect. Ask him or her to give you direction and help on how to connect the passion points in your life. Offer to become his or her shadow, so you can learn and build on knowledge. Find out what motivates this person and discover what you can do to help him or her. Raise your hand and ask for help. Raise your hand high and be explicit about what you need! Share your stories and dreams, and listen to his or her stories. I promise that you will make connections along this journey called life that will become part of your story and help you find your passion points.

Cultivate your passion points

- Why does being an adult often mean that you end up doing what you *don't* love? Embrace your passion; don't discount your dreams. Return to that childlike fascination you had with whatever it was, and find a way to spend your work and life passionately! Dial back to the passion of your teen years. What activities did you enjoy pursuing when you were 13 or 17 years old? Reflect back on those things you loved the most when you were growing up.

- Seek out passion partners (accountability partners) who will hold you to keep the promises you make to yourself. Who helps you stay accountable? In my life now, those people include my wife, my mother, my younger brother, and my son. Having someone who can help you honor the commitments you make, someone who is not jealous but who only wants the best for you, can be an invaluable resource.

- Share your story but be selective. Everyone, no matter what age, discovers at a certain point that he or she can share some stories, passions, and dreams with select people, and with others, not at all. Carefully choose those who you feel share your passions and interests. Reach out to your pastor or a teacher if all else fails.

- Write your dreams down in a journal, and search for books or other resources to spark your interests. If you find something that inspires you, share it with someone else. In this way you can help others find their passion points too.

3

Me, Inc.

● ●

When I joined Chase in 2000, a woman named Lisa Neal-Graves hired me. Lisa was a dynamic leader who made a quick impression on me with her unconventional approach. During one of our early meetings, Lisa offered some advice. She told me to try not to take the "platinum handcuffs." I had no idea what she was talking about and asked her to explain the concept. She said that the platinum handcuffs are considered some of the extra advantages that come with a job: the compensation, benefits, and perks that can slowly affect your judgment. They can cause you to compromise your beliefs, ignore your convictions, and ultimately lead you away from your best self when you indulge in them. The platinum handcuffs can influence you when it comes to making tough decisions or challenging certain people for fear that you might lose the "platinum" standing.

The sad part was watching how true her words were. As I began to pay attention to people's behavior, I found more examples where their decision-making was based on who they were aligned with (such as key influential people) and less about the merits of the issues being discussed.

That advice and my observations always stuck with me, so much so that over time and combined with my desire to protect our future, my wife and I agreed to try to save more by living below our means. We've been Christians for quite some time and are very used to tithing, but we also got into the habit of saving with the same discipline. We worked to modify our spending and ramped up my 401(k) contributions in order to take full advantage of saving more, sooner. This is particularly important given the Rule of 72. I'm not a financial advisor but the Rule of 72 is a simple financial lesson that stayed with me. It is merely a calculation to determine how long it will take your money to double. The calculation works as follows:

Take the amount of interest earned, such as 10 percent, and divide 10 into 72. That's roughly seven, which means your money will double in seven years. So in this example, if at age 20 you save $500 and invest it into something that yields 10 percent interest, you will have $1,000 by age 27. What's even more important is that it keeps growing. So in this same example, the following happens:

Age 20	Put in $500
Age 27	$1,000
Age 34	$2,000
Age 44	$4,000
Age 51	$8,000
Age 58	$16,000
Age 65	$32,000

This is how I began to think. It was important to put away as much as I could early on in order to get the Rule of 72 to work for our retirement. This mentality has helped to guide a lot of our personal spending decisions. In addition, my wife and I worked hard not to take on more debt than necessary, striving to pay down our mortgage as quickly as possible, and to pay with cash instead of credit as much as possible. This has allowed us to gain a lot of flexibility and not have to make decisions driven purely by finances.

When I got out of high school and after I was booted out of Temple University, I had an opportunity to work in a few recording studios. One studio I worked for was Preverbe Recording Studios located near 3rd and Market streets in Philadelphia. The owner, Robert "Taj" Walton, was a musician who became a great mentor. Though I was familiar with working in a studio, given some previous experience, Taj was particular about how his studio was run. He was very demanding, especially regarding the intricacies related to the recording sessions and those of his key clients.

Over time, Taj allowed me to run the studio solo, booking sessions for various groups that came to record. We had everything from rap to rhythm and blues and reggae. As my personal relationship developed with Taj, I couldn't help but notice that the studio was not making tons of cash. However, I also noticed that Taj never seemed terribly worried about it. He drove a nice car, had a nice home in Delaware, and could come and go as he pleased.

One day, I mustered up the courage to ask him how he supported himself, as the studio didn't produce a lot and I never heard him talk about having another job. He told me that

> *Money won't create success; the freedom to make it will.*
> —Nelson Mandela

he invested in real estate and owned several properties that he rented out. Ah, I thought, that made sense. It didn't hit me then, but Taj was truly living the dream. He worked and continued to invest in real estate to create the freedom to pursue his passion—music! Here we are some 20 or more years later and Taj is still doing just that, pursuing his passion.

Protect your legacy

In 2009, Tony Glover took over a part of the Chase credit card division, replacing Heather Phillip (who originally hired me into Chase Credit Card Services). Naturally, as a new leader, Tony needed to assess the area for which he had just accepted responsibility. Over the course of a few months, Tony did just that. He considered the organizational structure, the underlying strategy, and the talent needed to move the business forward. When he felt ready to take action, Tony spoke to me about the potential changes he needed to make, including a reduction in staff. One afternoon, Tony asked me to come down to his office to explain that he would be making some changes. He needed me to communicate this to those folks within the next two days. As you can imagine, this was a difficult moment. Whether you know it is coming or not, and even if you have dealt with staff reductions previously, informing people that they are losing their jobs is never easy.

Tony went on to explain other needed organizational changes, including a change in my role. His intention was to move me laterally into a different position. That is, although I would remain Senior Vice President, my responsibilities would be changing. The challenge for me was that this new position was a misuse or under-usage of my capabilities. This new position would not utilize my potential and could be damaging to my career and personal brand. Our conversation went something like this:

Tony: I have created a role for you that is of great importance to the company as we redefine how we think about the right partners for the company. You've clearly demonstrated the ability to do this work and I would like you to lead our partner rationalization work in a more focused way.

Me: True. However, it doesn't appear to give me significant growth-oriented work. I worry about not being aligned with what is truly important for the organization, which is revenue growth.

Tony: It is important work. You'll knock it out of the park, and then be able to do something else that is progressive.

Me: I really need to think about it overnight.

Tony: I need to have an agreement from you now—that you are moving into this role—because some communications will start tomorrow.

Me: Given everything we've just discussed about the people I need to lay off, getting my head around that and being prepared for those discussions, is enough for right now. I need time to properly think through the next part about my job.

Tony: We need to come to an agreement tonight.

Me: Tell you what. Given my years of commitment to this company and the fact that, in most of those years, I have been a top performer (and feel free to check my records as we are still getting to know each other), I believe I deserve another option. The job you are presenting to me is like asking Michael Jordan to be a second string guard and not a starter. I think that could have a long-lasting effect on my reputation, as well as on my career potential. I ask that you put another option on the table in terms of a leave package for me—a severance package.

Tony: You don't want to do that.

Me: I don't want to damage my future either, and I don't want to just "take a job" that is less than I know I can do and may potentially damage my future.

Tony and I agreed that we were not going to settle the issue that evening. We both went home.

As I arrived at the office early the next morning (both Tony and I typically arrived for work at 6:45 a.m.), Tony asked me to come down to his office. He explained that he had reconstructed the role a bit, with the addition of a number of affinity partnership responsibilities. It was a much more appealing position and a bit exciting. Though I was glad he had reconsidered my responsibilities, I didn't want to jump too quickly. I asked Tony why he had made the changes. He told me that, given the convictions I had expressed the night before, he was compelled to rethink things. He had spoken with his boss and had concluded that he needed to give me more opportunities in my next role. Great outcome!

So, what did I learn from this? Here are a few of the highlights:

- Creating financial flexibility allows you to trust and follow your passion. I knew that I was on a journey toward a CEO or COO (chief operating officer) role and that his proposed change in my responsibilities would be a step in the wrong direction for a number of reasons. More importantly, I had created the financial flexibility that allowed me to say "no" and negotiate.

- You have to protect your legacy and your reputation. Legacy sometimes sounds like a big word, but it boils down to what people think about you and what they will remember about you. I don't have all the words to describe how I want to be remembered, but I know that "stagnant" or "going backward" would not be included.

- It's important to let people know you have boundaries. It's not enough for you to know your passion and the plans you have, as you will face times where you will have to let others understand them as well. You need to be prepared to take a stand.

- Taking those challenging stances often makes you feel like you might put yourself and the relationship with the other party at risk. However, I have found that to be far from the truth. In fact, I believe this was one of those moments that helped me establish a stronger relationship with Tony that we still enjoy to this day, years later!

Understand that the right to choose your own path is a sacred privilege. Use it. Dwell in possibility.
—Oprah Winfrey

This statement from Oprah Winfrey shows that it's powerful to choose your own path. To do this, you have to prepare. In my case, this preparation took the form of choosing to save a percentage of my earnings. This allowed me the freedom to stand up for what I believed at work, rather than be forced to accept a position I didn't feel would be in my best interest. Because I wasn't tied to the "platinum handcuffs," I was able to make a decision based on what was important to me and what I felt passionate about. Making the lateral move that Tony originally suggested did not work for Rosseau, Inc., if you know what I mean! When you create a flexible life, you are not chained by your obligations. Instead, your possibilities are bolstered by your savings. Later in this chapter, we'll consider how you can create your own "Me, Inc."

Invest in yourself

Like most kids, my interests were all over the place when I was younger. I joined Cub Scouts and signed up for other clubs and lessons. My mom made the financial investment required for each endeavor and, as is also typical of most kids, my interests rapidly faded. After this happened a few times, my mother took action. She reminded me of my scattered interests and hobbies, informing me that, from then on, I would have to invest in these interests myself. This vital lesson on the importance of investing in myself has stayed with me throughout my life. I confess, I was a bit mad at her at the time, but now I am so thankful. It really taught me the value of having a vested interest in the things you want to do. It started at the age of 10 and grew into my future desire to save big so that I could continue to dream big. It is so important to continually invest in yourself. It establishes the discipline of identifying what is important to you, particularly in the long-term, as many investments don't have an immediate return.

Protect your passion points

While you're saving and investing, you should simultaneously start and continue to figure out where your passions intersect with your potential. By potential, I am referring to things that that stem from your natural gifts and talents.

One summer, I spent months trying to learn how to cut records on my mother's stereo unit—you know, the big one, with the TV in the middle, the phonograph player on one side, and the volume controls all the way down the other side. Mind you, these were coveted stereo entertainment units back in the day. But let's just say this was just not at all conducive for learning how to DJ.

At that time, there was a popular group in our neighborhood that I used to track behind. They were called the Grandmasters of Funk or something like that—bear with me; this was ages ago. The DJ, Duck, headed off to college, and he left his cherished turntables with his front man (emcee), Mark Bennett, who lived just a few houses down from me. I negotiated with Mark (okay, I begged) to borrow one of those turntables to learn on. He agreed and it was on!

I loved it. It just felt like something I absolutely should be doing, and I was now fully determined to become a DJ. Coincidentally, about this same time, my trumpet was in my uncle's car. It was stolen when his car was vandalized. So, when he got the insurance money, instead of replacing the trumpet, I was going to put those dollars toward some studio-type turntable equipment. But I was a little short of cash.

As I stated, my mother had seen me determined before to become a lot of things, so she wasn't full of inspiration to go and buy me the turntables I desperately wanted. Of course, I didn't want just any turntables, either. I wanted Technique 1200s. For a DJ, these were the ultimate turntables for cutting, scratching, and mixing. As I shared in Chapter 2, this was the catalyst that led to getting my first job at the hardware store.

During my high school years, I really got into more organized music recordings, acting as DJ and exploring my passion for music. At that time, there were a lot of up-and-coming rap groups across the city, and my high school had no lack of folks desiring to be on that long list. At various times during the day, whether at lunch or unofficial breaks in the hallway, you could often catch a rap session going on, with rappers just free-styling to show their skills.

Within the neighborhood, I had developed a decent reputation as a DJ, spinning at local parties. I had a crew of several emcees who would go with me to the parties and rap. We even developed some nice songs and skits as well. Over time, the crew dwindled down to just a few. My man Lamar Manson (now known as Black Ice for those who follow the spoken word circuit, like Def Jam Poetry) and I had developed a great relationship and started working on some songs. I met an assistant (Mr. D.) at my high school. He was also into the music business, and *voilà*, a music venture was formed. We worked with Mr. D. to produce a single that we recorded and released through the record label, Butterfly Records, which he and his partners owned. It was a great time, hearing our record on the radio, doing shows with well-known groups, and even doing some touring regionally. It never broke big time, but it did lead to other things, allowing me to work within the music industry in the Philadelphia area.

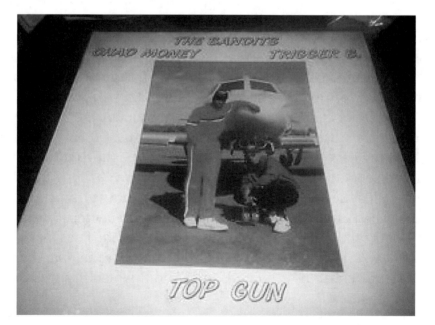

Though the music business never really took Lamar or me to the big time, we both landed in good places in terms of doing something we enjoy. I could mention many others from the music industry, such as artists and groups I worked with over the 20 years I've been involved, who ended up in similar situations.

An investment in knowledge pays the best interest.
—Benjamin Franklin

I used to ask myself, "Why aren't we making it?" There are a number of reasons I've come up with. Maybe our songs weren't catchy enough, or our label didn't push us right, or the beats weren't hot enough, or the act wasn't that special, or it was bad timing, poor promotion, or some combination. The list goes on and on. The point is the music career didn't take off. Although I could make the case that maybe we didn't work hard enough and keep at it, another side of me recalls that there is always a greater plan at work. Drive on!

Educate yourself

Another key investment is education. I believe that learning is a continuous process and a formal education is a part of that process. As mentioned earlier, I was highly disappointed that I initially could not attend college. I did other things like going right into the working world. However, after working for several years, I went back to school at night to complete my bachelor's degree at the tender age of 33. I recently started the Executive MBA program at Kellogg and have plans for a doctorate. I will be the first to say that going to school while working full-time is very challenging. Many of my colleagues and friends told me it was not worth it. In their minds, I had already achieved a high level of success. But school was important to me. Your education is one of the few things that no one can take from you. I have also found that the more I learn, the more I realize how much I don't know, which inspires me to learn even more!

As highlighted by many news stories, it has become clear that a high school education is not enough to get you into higher-paying jobs. Thus, many young people are finding ways to obtain a bachelor's degree. It appears, though, that the bar is being raised again. The competitive environment in today's corporate America is fierce. So unless you have experience that helps you stand out or otherwise offsets the lack of degree, it's become clear that you need a master's degree to succeed.

> *Imagine what a harmonious world it could be if every single person, both young and old, shared a little of what he is good at doing.*
> −Quincy Jones

Read, read, read

One of the things I have consistently done over the course of my career is reading all kinds of books by different types of authors. Whether it was Stephen Covey, Peter Drucker, or other inspirational authors, reading and learning about topics that included management or leadership were of huge interest to me. I found that the lessons I learned from these books helped me formulate my approach to different issues and situations in the workplace. I discovered that reading about another person's experience and thoughts on dealing with a particular issue in a similar situation often equipped me with new strategies. Even though I was experiencing something for the first time, the insights and lessons from others enriched my collection of possible responses and tactics. After all, you need to be open to learning from the mistakes of others. Life is too short to make all of the mistakes by yourself!

Be genuine and share yourself

I have had the opportunity to work with a wide variety of people thus far in my career. From some, I have learned things to do, and from others, things not to do. I can't recommend highly enough an approach that focuses on being a student of life and being willing to learn from mistakes, both your own and others'.

Life is what happens to you while you're busy making other plans.
—Allen Saunders

One of the things that I most appreciate from those who have willingly shared their mistakes is their attitude. These are people who believed in what they did, were passionate about it, and really cared. These are people who, in essence, do not fake being genuine. Maintaining this authenticity and integrity when sharing experiences speaks volumes about the person and magnifies the lessons that he or she is willing to share.

These experiential lessons bring into focus ways to make sure the work you are doing, first, matters to you; second, sparks your motivation; and third, makes you feel good. If the work—stripped of the money and prestige—makes you feel good, then you are on the right track. If you like dealing with wood and carpentry, be a carpenter. No matter how much money you can make in plumbing or how much status you can get as a painter, if your passion is in carpentry, you are not going to get the same energy and feeling by being a painter.

If you approach your work from this perspective, recognizing what you like and don't like, you will not only point yourself in the right direction, you'll also realize that no job or career will ever be perfect. There will always be pros and cons. Your key task is to make sure the pros outweigh the cons. Once you set your mind to approach life with this healthy mindset, it will naturally affect how you interact with the people you deal with, both professionally and personally. You'll begin to care deeply about your work, your surroundings, and the company you keep. You'll begin to think more about the collective victories rather than focusing solely on your own personal gains. That is a great and powerful lesson to learn as early as possible—understanding that when the team wins, you win too.

Be prepared for change

As I look back over my career and the various jobs I have had, from the hardware store until now, I am reminded that I did not plan to be in most of them. What is equally interesting to me is that those things that I did plan to do often did not pan out. When I was younger, I just knew I was going to be an architect; then, I was going to be a professional athlete; then, I was going to be a CFO; then, I was going to be an artist and music producer. I think you get the point.

What I have learned is that life "happens," and the events that occur can often supersede or alter your plan. That said, though it is okay and in fact prudent to create career goals and plans, do not be so wedded to them as to refuse to see, seize, or capitalize on any other opportunities that may unfold. That is the meaning behind the well-known phrase "If life gives you lemons, make lemonade!"

Private practice enhances public performance

I have always been drawn to those people who are so passionate about what they do—no matter what industry—that they simply stand out among a sea of talent. The common denominator is work ethic. Those gifted individuals are not content to rest on the laurels of physical strength, mental ability, or past accomplishments. These stars also work incredibly hard to hone their skills. When I was playing football in junior high and high school, I remember how focused I was on being one of the best. At the time, I was hoping to be a great fullback, and so I worked very hard at it. I was constantly managing my weight to ensure I made the weigh-ins, working on my speed, fitting in extra workouts, and whatever else I could do. I kept a sharp eye on those who I thought were phenomenal at the sport. For me, there was one player who stood out from the rest: Walter Payton. I remember how much I enjoyed watching him play and marveled at how amazing and gifted he was.

I still remember watching an extended interview with Payton, which showed his workout regimen during the off-season—you know, that time of year when the football players were supposed to be off. It was incredible. His workout routine was almost as rigorous as the regular season team workouts, if not more so. If you ever check out any articles about Walter Payton, he is always noted as having a grueling solo off-season workout program. This helped me figure out early on the importance of what Stephen Covey says in his must-read book, *The 7 Habits of Highly Effective People*, "Private victories always precede public victories." The people around you will see how you do in the actual race, but most won't see you practice, as there is no thrill in that. However, you must put in the time to train and prepare if you want to compete well. Practice is the key and will determine how well you do in the actual game.

Develop and invest in Me, Inc.

We all have dreams and visions of what we'd like to accomplish in this life. Often, our best-laid plans are cast aside when we come up against the obstacles and challenges that life sends our way. Despite my disappointment at various crossroads, I do believe that I've managed to seize opportunities and create moments that set me on the road of my life. I similarly want to encourage you to seize the opportunities that present themselves so that you can step onto your road for the best life you can lead. If you have a passion point that you want to pursue, it is imperative that you protect and develop it. Absent any fire-retardant, fortress-like protection, passion and the pursuit thereof can die underneath the weight of everyday realities.

Here are some ways you can develop the tools you'll need to purposely gear up for the journey ahead:

- Create flexibility in your life by proactively choosing to save instead of spend.
- Build a discipline around saving.

- Protect your legacy, what you want to be known for, and what you stand for.

- Figure out where your passion, skills, and gifts intersect. This is your point of highest leverage.

- Read a diverse collection of books and authors.

- Cultivate genuineness, caring, and sharing.

- Don't react. Be prepared and proactive.

- Practice, practice, practice.

4

Promise 2: Perform to Progress

• •

This chapter sets the stage for Promise 2, which is to perform to progress. As it relates to resources, there is typically more demand than supply and that requires prioritization. In this chapter we'll discuss some key ways in which you can set yourself apart by prioritizing, innovating, and promoting with purpose.

During my early days at Chase, the head of HR was John Farrell. I didn't get a chance to know John as well as I would have liked, but I did get to spend some time with him in group sessions, as well as a few one-on-ones. He was an unconventional coach. Although he understood the need to manage through corporate politics, he always seemed to have a different take on things. He would often use the analogy that, in baseball, if you batted .300 (which means you hit almost one third of your times at bat) you were a hero and that if you batted .700 in the Chase culture, we'd yell, "You suck." That point stuck with me because John underscored the value of making progress as you move through your career.

One person who comes to mind with regards to continually making progress is a fictional character: James Evans from *Good Times*. I know he is a character from a TV show, but for me, particularly as an African-American male, he was a tremendous role model. *Good Times* was a TV show that originally came on the air in 1974 and ran through 1979. I watched it as a kid and to this day, whenever it comes on TV, I tape episodes on our DVR. In fact, my family knows I like it so much that my mother purchased me the DVDs a year or two ago. Though a lot of African-American TV shows have been aired through the years, many of which I enjoy, this one remained with me, as it epitomizes determination and progress amidst struggle.

James Evans (played by actor John Amos) is the father and Florida Evans (who firmly instilled Christian values and was played by actress Esther Rolle) was the mother. Their three children are the teenaged J.J. and Thelma, and 11-year-old Michael.

The family of five lived in a two-bedroom, one-bathroom apartment in the Chicago projects, surviving in spite of their poverty. They would often joke about the broken elevator, less-than-functioning laundry room, and having to step over drunken street people to make their way home.

I always liked what I saw in James Evans and, though I've seen every episode dozens of times, I tend to watch the ones prior to him dying off the show a lot more. James had a difficult upbringing; when he was just a young boy, his father went to the store to get some groceries and never came back home. No letters, no phone calls—he just never came back. Although they never fully connect the dots, this is probably tied to why James never achieved more than a sixth grade education. He was a man of pride who often stated that he would not accept charity.

James had a singular passion: providing a better way of life for his family. Through the episodes, you see him working two to three jobs at once (dishwasher, car wash attendant, loading dock worker, construction laborer, and so on), going back to school to get his GED (General Educational Development), and constantly striving to move forward. He even gets into an apprenticeship program and takes a job in Alaska, hoping to send money back to the family. Though he didn't have a formal education, he fought to ensure his children did, and he diligently worked to make sure his eldest, J.J., could pursue his art career; that his daughter, Thelma, could pursue her dreams of dance; and that their youngest, Michael, could pursue his dreams of becoming a Supreme Court justice.

There were times when the family could have taken shortcuts, such as when they could have kept money that they found from a bank robbery. Despite their tremendous need, however, they turned it in to the authorities. Even though they often didn't have two nickels to rub together themselves, if they saw someone in need, they would figure out a way to help.

I loved what I saw in James Evans and, as much as I missed him on the show, I loved what I saw in John Amos, the actor who played his character. Amos reportedly left the show over a disagreement with its direction. He believed the show had lost its original intent, which was to deal with meaningful content.

> *The ship's captain cannot see his destination for fully 99 percent of his journey—but knows what it is, where it is, and that he will reach it if he keeps doing certain things a certain way.*
> *—Dennis Kimbro*

It says a lot to me as an African-American male that John Amos went into doing the show to make progress relative to the quality of television for African Americans and that he had the courage to risk being fired from it for the same reason. For over three decades this show has been a staple for me, helping me stay grounded in what's important and the fact that the "how" is as equally important as the "what."

Choose progress over perfection

Most of us have experienced, at one time or another, the reality that perfection—or the pursuit of it—can often lead to paralysis. Instead of striving for perfection, try this as an alternative: base your performance around making progress toward your big goals, dreams, and visions, while celebrating each small step along the way.

As I have noted before, passion is the first promise. It is a key ingredient in the larger process of fueling your progress. Unfortunately, the world doesn't reward dreamers for dreaming, but for doing. You must always challenge yourself to perform at the highest possible level, seeking to make progress with each new skill set you learn and every action you take. *You can die striving for perfection, but you can live well when you focus on making progress.*

Differentiation versus performance

In his book, Mojo, best-selling management and leadership author Dr. Marshall Goldsmith says that a great leader understands the difference between "smart" and "effective." He points out that smart people tend to work hard to show that they are very intelligent. However, emerging leaders soon discover that this approach doesn't work well as they continue to climb the corporate ladder. Peers will likely see them as boasters and so avoid interacting with them. The effective approach, on the other hand, is to engage with others by asking open-ended questions and sharing what matters most to them. In turn, these empathic leaders become sought after for their ability to listen and connect well with peers. As author and Wharton professor Arthur Grant points out in his book, *Give and Take*, these types of people will be seen as "Givers" versus "Takers." As such, they are ensured more success in their careers.

The following skills will help you maximize your own, as well as others' performance:

- **Self-awareness.** Be aware of your emotions and how they affect you and those around you. Take notice of what causes you stress and how you deal with it.

- **Self-expression.** This involves being able to express how you feel, both verbally and non-verbally. It is important that you can communicate openly, in an assertive and acceptable manner. If you find you have a hard time saying no, practice establishing boundaries and learn how to engage in healthy conflict. (*The Power of a Positive No* by William Ury offers great insights into this idea.)

- **Interpersonal relationships.** This skill involves developing and keeping relationships that are characterized by mutual trust, understanding, and consideration. Work on your ability to share what other people are going through (without getting caught up in the drama) and staying calm when others may show strong emotions.

- **Decision-making.** This is the ability to be objective by seeing things as they really are. You can solve problems objectively, and keep your emotions and reactions in check when dealing with input from others.

- **Stress tolerance.** This involves coping with difficult situations in a positive way. It is an attitude that is hopeful, despite setbacks, and a viewpoint that strives to seek balance in all aspects—mental, emotional, and physical.

One way to think about progress is with differentiation and performance. This is about finding and pursuing an authentic way to distinguish yourself among your peers. It's about doing the unexpected or performing beyond the average or even choosing to take the squiggly line rather than the straight line. This last path is probably the most thought provoking.

> *We can make ourselves miserable or we can make ourselves strong— the amount of work is the same.*
> —Carlos Castaneda

For example, let's imagine you're my son, and I give you a dollar and say, "I'd like some ice cream. Go to the ice cream store," and you bring back a couple of scoops of ice cream. You've brought me ice cream and that's good, just what I expected. But what if you came back with a hot fudge sundae, loaded with whipped cream and nuts? Somehow you've gotten more than what's expected, thereby setting yourself apart. You may have told the shop owner that your father is a patron of this shop and it is his favorite place for ice cream. The next time you go to the store for ice cream, you mention how wowed your father was with all of those extra toppings and, soon, you find that every time you return to the store, you get a little something extra. This is an example of wowing on a whole new level. You have now gone above and beyond, making a "wow event" sustainable.

Perform progressively, look for "additives"

The process where you consistently achieve the "wow" is how I would characterize performing progressively. There are a number of tools to help you perform progressively on a regular basis, including prioritization and innovation. Setting priorities can power your progression as seen in the following story.

Ordinary things consistently done produce extraordinary results.

—*Keith Cunningham*

A colleague of a friend was the head of marketing for a top hotel chain. During one particularly difficult time, while the entire Italian soccer team was staying at the hotel during the World Cup, her staff kept coming to her with complaints. After several days of constant interruptions and non-stop complaints, she finally found a way to stop the madness. She simply stated, "If you want to come in and complain about anything, please first take the time to figure out at least two options to address the complaints. You can prioritize and share these along with the complaint. In this way, we can get much more done, in a faster period of time."

By encouraging her staff to prioritize their suggestions, she helped them focus on what was important–addressing issues in a timely manner–and also cut down on the non-stop interruptions. Prioritization used to be one of my weakest skills. What did I do to compensate? I surrounded myself (and still do) with people who do it exceptionally well.

Innovate

Innovation enjoys a preeminent place in your quest to achieve consistent progress. With innovation, the emphasis is on doing one thing or a number of things that haven't been done before, with the goal of making a big impact. When I was at JPMorgan Chase as HR service delivery executive for North America, we were looking at numerous ways to be more efficient while at the same time striving to improve our services.

We found that one of the areas in which employee dissatisfaction reigned was in the replacement of lost payroll checks. Numerous issues fed into this problem. Whether it was our dependence on the U.S. postal system, printer issues, or local distribution in buildings, the results were the same. Every payday, countless employees did not receive their checks. We launched an initiative to improve this problem.

Naturally, the first level of suggestions focused on fixing the specific elements of the process. In other words, get the U.S. postal system to do something special for us, or assign dedicated individuals in buildings across the country to hand-deliver paychecks. (Consider that we had more than 80,000 employees, and you'll see why this was not a crazy-good innovative idea.)

I challenged our team to work with our platform provider and think about electronic payments. You might imagine that people in the banking industry would take electronic payments in stride. Think again. This innovative solution created a small uproar. The thought of asking all employees to take payments by direct deposit caused quite a stir. The sheer enormity of shifting the behavior of those who relied on the security of holding a physical check was overwhelming. At that time, no organization of our size or prominence had done it. However, we decided to dig in our heels and get it done. It was important for this project, and it would help us progress as a culture and move our leadership and employees into the digital age.

Promote with purpose

During the transitioning to electronic payments, I encountered several barriers—cultural, philosophical, and legal, among others. The pushback reached such an extreme that the initial project manager, who reported to me, became insubordinate and eventually exited the company. However, 12 months later, we implemented the electronic payroll system, with rapid adoption company-wide. After our successful conversion in the United States, JPMorgan Chase began adopting the practices around the globe. In the United States, we helped lead the way for implementing an electronic timekeeping system, and several manager and employee self-service systems. This was a complete cultural and digital improvement from just five years before.

The man with insight enough to admit his limitations comes nearest to perfection.
—*Goethe*

As a result of my involvement in the switch to electronic payments, I was asked to coauthor an article in *Paytech*, the magazine of the American Payroll Association. The piece was about innovation in the field. In addition to writing the article, I was also invited to speak at a number of industry conferences. This experience helped me make progress toward my promises in several ways. I pursued my passion in innovation. I performed to progress by creating something that didn't exist before. I promoted with purpose. I was able to leverage the accomplishments to further expose my personal brand, both internally and externally. I parlayed my platform, leveraging the accomplishments in order to expand my roles. I'll talk more about these two elements in later chapters.

Tools to help set you apart

Good workers are always essential to a company's success. Given today's uncertain economy, it is more important than ever that you do what you can to be in demand. Being valued as a strong contributor will increase your chances of promotion or advancement. Here are some ways in which you can stand out:

- **Become a specialist.** If you're the one person in your group who possesses a specific skill, you can improve your value to your employer by continuing to build on that strength. For example, if you're the only team member knowledgeable in a software program or who is familiar with certain rules and regulations of a country where an important client is based, make sure you keep that knowledge current. Keep up with the updates, take classes, and, in general, maintain your edge by keeping any certifications or requirements up to date.

  An essential aspect of being a specialist is to share what wisdom you have. Let others know your area of expertise and that you're available if needed. By helping others, you can become that go-to person and a very valuable resource within your organization.

- **Display integrity.** Don't be afraid to voice your concerns or question something that doesn't feel right. It can be easy to get carried away with the "but we've always done it this way" mentality. Instead, listen to your gut if something seems unusual or questionable, or doesn't feel right to you. Research the issue and dig deeper. You may discover a problem before it becomes a major nightmare for the organization later on.

- **Improve visibility.** No matter where you are in the company's hierarchy, you can make others aware of your strengths. It is possible to let others (especially those who make the decisions on key factors) know of your accomplishments without running around tooting your own horn. The best way is to take advantage of opportunities to displaying your talents while getting to know different people throughout the company. For example, you can volunteer to work on cross-functional teams, or help professionals or colleagues in a different department. The more people who know about your skill set, the more chances you may find to show off your responsibilities.

    We'll explore other ways to effectively improve your visibility with networking in Chapter 9. I'll just mention here that networking applies to all aspects of your life, not just during work hours. Annual picnics, holiday parties, and other social functions are great ways to meet others across the organization and strengthen your working relationships.

- **Choose to lead.** You don't have to be a manager or a supervisor to take on leadership responsibilities. Do your coworkers and peers often ask for your help or advice? If so, that's because you are demonstrating leadership abilities. It shows that others trust your judgment and respect your skills. You can continue to develop these leadership qualities by honing your skills and by serving as a mentor to others.

    Only you have the power to influence how people at a company think of you. The more employees and managers consider you as indispensable, the more likely you will remain a productive member of your organization, especially during turbulent economic times.

Dream with your eyes open

Dreaming with our eyes open on the journey toward the passion point also means acknowledging the current environment that we are in. In this environment, performance is a mighty differentiator that helps drive priorities. Let's review some of the ways you can set yourself apart in order to perform progressively toward your dreams:

- Think differently from those around you. Set yourself apart by learning new skills and further developing those abilities that help you stand out.

- Progress, not perfection, should be your constant mantra. The goal should always be to keep moving forward, even if that means taking small steps, one at a time. If you get caught up in striving for perfection, you may give up in frustration before attaining your goals.

- Innovate: there's a better way to get things done. Think outside the box and think of projects or situations that will help you progress, both personally and professionally. When I encouraged my team to undertake the concept of direct deposit for our employees, it moved our company and my professional career forward into the digital age.

- Promote your skills with purpose similar to how I was able to leverage my professional accomplishments to further expose my brand, both internally and externally. In Chapter 11, I will discuss in more detail the different ways you can expand your role and parlay your platform.

5

Persistent Progression Club

• •

Membership has its privileges, even on this journey. Maintaining your good standing in the persistent progression club can serve as an EZ-Pass for your career by providing access to the fast lane, getting you through life's tolls easily and quickly. This chapter provides tools to help define, reach, monitor, and sustain membership in the persistent progression club. I've included a major milestone story: when I moved from the banking industry to Allstate, a Fortune 50 company. If I had not made a commitment to move on, I would still be in a job where I likely would have started slipping from the club. I was in a situation at the bank with everything under control, as though I was in maintenance mode. As I've gotten to know myself, I've discovered that I become bored during this stage. I need challenge. I need a learning curve career path. I thrive on performance.

After a series of what I considered to be major achievements—including a major systems implementation, the JPMorgan Chase/ Bank One merger and the migration of my functions from New York to Delaware, and completing the transition to electronic pay statements—I thought I was doing well. I was still the payroll director and was comfortable in my role. However, not long after I moved,

I began reporting to a different manager, Jennifer Cavazzini. Prior to this, Jennifer and I had been peers and colleagues, but she was a more seasoned manager than I was at the time. As soon as I was notified of the reporting relationship change, Jennifer and I began having conversations about how we could work best together. Her plan was not to interfere too heavily, but to let me continue to operate rather autonomously, as she felt I demonstrated good performance. In return, I asked her to give me frequent feedback to ensure I got the benefit of her experience.

> *If you put yourself in a position where you have to stretch outside your comfort zone, then you are forced to expand your consciousness.*
>
> —Les Brown

Through time, I noticed that in large group meetings, particularly during visits from our senior executive, Debbie Bealle, Jennifer began pushing me to lead the sessions. I didn't understand why she did this. In fact, I was totally irritated! I was an introvert—as determined through Myers-Briggs testing. I didn't see the need to be up in front of a group of 100 or so folks. Jennifer was the leader of the HR service delivery Delaware team. In my mind, she should have been the one leading. Yet time and time again, Jennifer insisted. Guess what? I got better and more comfortable with leading the sessions. Within six months, Jennifer retired and I got promoted to her position. It was then that I connected all the dots. Jennifer believed I had great leadership capabilities, but I also needed to be comfortable "physically," leading the team with presence. Her decision to push me to lead the sessions provided me with the opportunities to develop that skill set.

This experience was a motivating factor in changing my behavior. I began not only to seek opportunities to develop within myself, but also to reach out beyond my comfort zone. I became like a whirlwind as I:

- Asked my manager to lead a global initiative to optimize our payroll and data management for more than 30 countries.

- Suggested that there was an opportunity to optimize all of our HR service delivery efforts in North America and that I wanted to lead it. (I was fortunate to get the role.)

- Went back to school to earn my bachelor's degree (completing it at the tender age of 33).

- Stepped forward in a very different way to lead a number of efforts in the JPMorgan Chase/Bank One merger.

- Sought to make a major career change from HR service delivery, which was largely an operations and services function, toward a more revenue-generating role within the firm.

After 11 years at JPMorgan Chase and Financial Services, including my move from operations and services to a revenue-generation function, I was thoroughly excited to leave and join Allstate to learn a very different industry. What I find most interesting now is my attitude concerning performance. Make no mistake: I want to win and win big! But I find myself equally focused on questions like "What am I learning?" and "Am I personally growing through the work I am involved in?" That is equal to, if not more important than, just winning. I not only realized the importance of persistent progression, but also of consistent progression. I embraced the concept of finding learning curves and opportunities to stretch myself.

We cannot become what we want to be by remaining what we are.
—Max DePree

Understand where you are on the learning curve

There is a process that was developed by Noel Burch, an employee of Gordon Training International in the 1970s. It is still taught today. The premise is that there are essentially four stages of learning required for any new skill. The stages provide a model for learning. They include:

- **Stage 1: Unconscious Incompetence.** In this first stage, you may not recognize that you are lacking a skill. You may not be aware that the new skill exists. You don't understand why it could be important to learn it. Before you can move on to the second stage, you need to be aware of your lack of skill. It also requires that you want to fill the knowledge gap.

- **Stage 2: Conscious Incompetence.** At this stage, you realize the necessity for acquiring the missing skill and make an effort to acquire knowledge and practice of it. Failure is a big part of this stage. Get used to failing and getting back up to try again!

- **Stage 3: Conscious Competence.** At this stage, you have acquired the skills necessary but still need to concentrate in order to perform your best.

- **Stage 4: Unconscious Competence.** After enough experience and practice, the skill has become so easy that you don't have to think about it. Your confidence in your ability is evident, and you are now at a new, higher level of capability. (For more details, see: *www.gordontraining.com/free-workplace-articles/ learning-a-new-skill-is-easier-said-than-done/*.)

In addition to these four stages, I believe progression should continue into Stage 5, which has been identified by some as Super-Conscious Competence. Here, you don't slip into that unconscious state especially as related to the skill development areas that really matter. I place into this category the skills of building relationships and relationship networks, mentoring, team building, speaking, facilitating, training, and leadership, just to name a few. All these arenas hold the potential for new levels of personal and professional growth. Don't go unconscious around the skills that make the biggest difference.

Overcoming fear

We all have fears that constantly challenge us. Yours may be different from mine, but I have no doubt there are a number of fears we have in common. For example, many people have that stomach-rumbling fear that's associated with public speaking. I have experienced that, too, especially as it pertained to presentations in front of groups. But what we don't always understand is that fears that affect us outside the workplace can become startlingly relevant to our professional life. It is important to recognize and embrace your fears and focus on developing tools to overcome them.

For instance, let's take the fear of horseback riding. Believe it or not, that was one of my big fears and for a very good reason. When I was about 10 years old, I had a great opportunity to do some horseback riding with a group of folks in New York City–Central Park to be exact. It was a beautiful day. Upon arriving at the storage facility, we all mounted our horses and set out into Central Park. We were instructed to stay together as a group, with each of our horses following behind the one in front of us. The idea was for our horses to trot in a group through the park. However, my horse just wouldn't trot. Instead, he walked slowly. It wasn't long before my horse and I began to fall behind the rest of the group.

Courage is resistance to fear, mastery of fear; not absence of fear.
—Mark Twain

As I was new to horseback riding, I wasn't sure how to get the horse to pick up speed. I began to tighten the reins in my hands and snap them against the horse's neck, but it didn't affect him at all.

He just continued to walk. I then wrapped the reins tighter in my hand and kicked my heels along the horse's side as well—that did it. He took off running! There we were, running through Central Park, completely out of control. I grabbed a hold of his mane, terrified, with my glasses bouncing up and down on my face and my heart racing. Some of the adults from our group followed and tried to get the horse to slow down, but nothing seemed to work. The horse just ran and ran. About 15 minutes later, the fire department intervened. With their assistance, we were able to slow down the horse. They backed him into a corner, and I was able to jump off. The horse was taken back to the stables while I was left to catch my breath.

From that moment on, I developed an unbelievable fear of horses. I couldn't imagine riding one for pleasure. I became uncomfortable just being near a horse. Fast-forward to just a few years ago: I was on a business trip in Arizona with some colleagues. During the trip, my manager, Steve Hallett (a great friend to this day), had scheduled some time for team-building activities but he didn't specify the details. He wanted it to be a surprise. The group of us departed from the hotel for the team-building event, jumped into some vans, and headed out. On the way there, Steve unveiled the details. We were heading to the All-Star Ranch, a place where many professional players (that is, members of the NBA) leave their horses to be used as rental horses for charity. Surprise! We were going to be horseback riding together! I began to sweat profusely. I couldn't imagine getting on a horse again. I decided I would have to tell Steve and the team that I simply couldn't do it, and I would wait for them in the van. Then it hit me. Why not face my fear?

I remembered one of my favorite phrases from Stephen Covey's book *The 7 Habits of Highly Effective People*, which states, "Private victories precede public victories." I thought the whole thing through, from mounting the horse, to riding and dismounting. I asked myself this question throughout: "What's the worst that can happen?" So I made up my mind to do it. In my mind, it seemed easy enough, and then we arrived!

We pulled up at the ranch, exited the vehicles, and were greeted by an organizer from the facility. The organizer provided us with an overview of the facility and described what they do relative to supporting charities through the rental of horses. He and his team then began to bring out the horses. They were really beautiful. The team members brought each horse out of the trailer and assigned it to one of us. Each of us then mounted his horse and started to trot around a bit, to get a feel for the horse. There were about 10 of us in the group. As you might imagine, my anxiety grew with the introduction of each new horse. Naturally, I was the last in line to get one.

Finally, it was my turn. As I looked at the horse trailer, I knew the last one to emerge was for me. The black horse that stepped out of the trailer was larger than life, huge and muscular. I still can't believe how absolutely massive this horse was! The organizer then said to me, "Meet Barkley. This is Charles Barkley's horse, so we just call him Barkley." Struggling to move my legs and walk, I slowly put one foot in front of the other and walked over to Barkley. I reached up and patted him on the head saying, "Nice, Barkley." I was terrified. Not only was I trying to get over my historical fear of horses, I realized I had more than met my match with this colossal creature. He was massive—and massively worthy of my respect! He was so tall that they had to boost me up to get into the saddle.

We headed out on the group trail trip, and I'll admit, it was tough initially. The trail we were following went up and down mountainsides, along some very skinny trail lines. This caused Barkley to slip and slide a bit, driving me crazy, of course. However, about 20 minutes into the trail ride, I felt fine. When we finished the ride, I was more than fine. I was ecstatic. It felt great to finally face something I had avoided for more than 15 years of my life. From this experience, I was able to develop a process that I still use whenever I have to face a fear.

Facing the Fear Model

- See the beginning, middle, and end of the situation. I imagine myself going through it step by step.

- Size up the situation and describe it.

- Ask yourself, "How should I deal with this fear? Should I take it on or choose another path?"

- Ask, "What's the worst that can happen?" Here, I imagine the worst possible outcome and consider how I would deal with it.

Monitoring your progress

Monitoring and improving on your own work performance is one of the most effective ways you can persistently progress. After all, if you don't keep track of how you're doing, you won't know whether you're progressing in the right direction! By staying on top your work performance, you can:

- Get things done right the first time.

- Provide your best at all times, whether it be a service, a product, or a presentation that is free from errors, oversights, or defects.

- Reduce your need to "put out fires"–those situations that can be caused by a lack of planning or organization.

When you work inefficiently, you waste time and may even lose productivity, profitability, or goodwill. Here are some tips and techniques you can use to acquire good habits when it comes to monitoring your own performance:

- Always check your spelling before you print a document. Use your dictionary!

- Ask for feedback on your work from peers or coworkers so that you can get an honest idea of where you need to improve and what you can do differently.

- Use a "to-do" list or keep a schedule on your computer, laptop, or cell phone so that you don't miss important deadlines. I use a few different things. I often put things into buckets that I call the 4Ps (people, processes, platforms, and performance). From there, I create a quadrant-like scorecard and put the three or four most critical items for each bucket on paper. Next to each item I assign a due date, current status, and a RAG (red, amber, or green) for each item. (I discuss this system in more detail in Chapter 12.) I've developed a rhythm for reviewing each Friday afternoon. I block off time on my calendar to review incoming status reports from my team, due by noon each Friday, along with my own 4Ps report. This helps me plan my calendar and priorities for the following week.

- Keeping a work journal to write down any "tricks of the trade" or shortcuts you learn. This will become a valuable resource you can refer back to.

- Remember that your coworkers are often looking for solutions to the same problems you face. Consulting with others can trigger a creative solution that helps everyone.

Not everyone will recognize your progress

Don Fleming, one of my mentors who helped me move from security at Today's Man into the corporate offices, often shared his wisdom with me. One insight he shared is, "The best offer you get in a company is when you join the company. After that, it tends to be cost-of-living increases." At that time, I thought it was purely about compensation. Though that is clearly part of the point he was making, it was about much more than that.

Many people have a difficult time viewing you beyond their first impression. So to Don's point, although he could see the potential in the security guard, to many in the company, I was still "just a security guard." They had a hard time wrapping their heads around my progress. This didn't turn out to be debilitating to me at all. During my years of mentoring, I have seen many mentees face the same challenge of not seeing things around them (such as compensation, job titles) progress in line with the progress they were making relative to their skill sets, capabilities, and ultimately the contribution they are making to the company.

Sustaining your progress

We all need to realize the importance of reaching, monitoring, and sustaining our membership in the persistent progression club. If I had not made a commitment to switch organizations and even go into an all-new industry—from the bank to Allstate—I might still be lingering in a job where I was slipping from the club. Admittedly, given who I am, when I was in a situation akin to maintenance, with everything in a status quo state, I knew it would not last. I knew myself, and recognized my need for a challenge in a career that allows me the opportunity to continue to learn. I thrive on performance. Had I not been stretched from leading the group meeting sessions, I might not have considered public speaking as a possible venue for sharing my experiences, nor stepped into all the possibilities that awaited me once I got out of my comfort zone. Choosing to face my fears as they arise has had a huge impact on both my personal and professional life.

There is no question: people will see when you progress. They will note your consistency and they will appreciate your commitment to continuous development. Whether you are phenomenally successful in any particular instance is not the main point. Adaptability, resilience, and courage will strongly factor into your ability to sustain your progress in ways both big and small. I will talk much more about these elements and offer strategies and tactics to help you sustain your progress in Chapter 11. For now, let's look at some of the ways you can achieve and maintain good standing in the persistent progression club:

- Evaluate and understand where you are currently with your progress. Every club has its rules, and the rules of the persistent progression club insist that you keep up your membership by knowing where you stand. You are always on a learning curve, so keep in mind the five stages of competence as you stretch yourself with new experiences.

- Find tools that help you monitor your progress on a consistent basis. If you don't already, begin using a daily "to-do" list to keep you organized. Start a journal to track your progress. This will help drive you forward, and give you a chance to see where you've been and how far you've come.

- Consistently work on overcoming fears, as they can be debilitating to progress. Face your fears, realizing that overcoming them can be a valuable measure of your progress. When confronting a fear, size it up, describe it, and consider the worst-case scenario. Chances are the reality will be much tamer than what you imagine!

- Sustained cycles of progress create opportunities. The more you perform consistently and reliably with continuous development, the more people will notice. When you are adaptable and resilient, with the courage to face your fears, you will be prepared to accept new challenges and prospects as they come. The more prepared you are for opportunities, the more you can take advantage of them.

6

Managing Your GPS

● ●

We've discussed the importance of discovering your passion points and following your dreams with your eyes wide open, so let's take a look at *how* you're going to reach your ultimate goal. As in life, you can't reach your destination just by randomly driving around. You won't accomplish much by choosing haphazard turns in the road with no thought about the future. There is no "yellow brick road." In fact, you'll encounter obstacles no matter what road you choose. It might even seem like every road is paved with obstacles. Roadblocks, barriers, and learning curves are always present, so you need to learn how to navigate these detours along your journey. This chapter will provide insights to help you set up and manage a personal navigation system—your internal GPS—that will keep you on course, because there is no straight line to success.

Why so driven?

As I mentioned in Chapter 2, I had the opportunity to speak privately with the chairman and CEO of the company where I was then employed in a casual, relaxed setting. Though I had some interactions with Marvin "Skip" Schoenhals during regular workdays at WSFS, this was the first time I had a chance to catch up with him out of the office.

We talked about many recent accomplishments and how things were going for WSFS. He acknowledged quite a few of my efforts, which was very encouraging. During our conversation, he made references to something historical of which I had no knowledge. He looked at me with a quizzical gaze and asked me how old I was. I was in my 20s then. When I told him that, he was visibly startled. He looked as if he had a hard time believing that I'd taken on the responsibilities I had at such a young age. His words were along the lines of "I have a 24-year-old running part of HR for this company?" My response was, "Do you have any concerns about my work, or are you happy with it?" He responded that he was happy with it, and we both shared a good laugh.

He then asked, "Why do you push and work so hard to do all of the things you are doing?" It was then that one of my passions became crystal clear to me. My reply was, "I want to be able to show people from the neighborhood that you don't have to be a rapper, play basketball, or sell drugs in order to make it." The words may have been a little different, but that was the main thrust of it. That phrase took us into a deeper conversation. I told Skip that one day I wanted to go back into the neighborhood, driving a Lexus, showing them that I did it—achieved the symbols of success—but in a different way. More importantly, the intent of my message was that such success was achievable for them as well. I wanted to help people see their way out of what they probably considered a destiny they were stuck with.

That passion has served me well as a GPS point. Throughout my journey, it has often been less about particular roles, titles, or industries, and more about growing. I've also found that knowing where I want to go, and expressing my convictions and passion have also opened doors for me. That one conversation with the CEO was a catalyst for a change in direction in my life. Skip introduced me to venture capitalists on the bank's board, and he participated in helping me work through some goals I was trying to accomplish.

Your brain is an internal GPS

Just like you enter a new address into your car's or smartphone's GPS, you can also enter new destinations into your internal GPS–your brain. Instead of a new physical direction, you can modify your brain to create something different in your life. It may be a new skill, a new job, or a new way to behave. One of the biggest differences between the GPS in the car and your brain is how easy it is to program your car! It is fairly simple to enter a new address and go on your way. However, the internal GPS takes time, energy, and consistent dedication.

The target you program into your brain is your vision for how you'd like your life to be. It is imperative that you are clear on what you want, because your brain already has a destination programmed into it–which is your current life. You know that expression "Insanity: doing the same thing over and over again and expecting different results." When you want different results,

If you're trying to achieve, there will be roadblocks. I've had them; everybody has had them. But obstacles don't have to stop you. If you run into a wall, don't turn around and give up. Figure out how to climb it, go through it, or work around it.
—Michael Jordan

you have to program in a new destination. Once you have added a new aim into your internal GPS, you can begin following those new directions.

When you know what you want to do and can say it clearly, people will hear you and will then add their resources to yours. You have to know how to articulate your thoughts clearly and be willing to share your stories and passions. When you do that, then you will engage the passions and connections of your colleagues, coaches, and mentors as well.

Roadblocks, barriers, and learning curves along the way

Challenges are inevitable as we move forward in life, but most challenges we deal with go hand-in-hand with obstacles that interfere with–and sometimes even prevent–our progress. As you pursue your goals, you will inevitably come face to face with big, overwhelming impediments along the way. How you deal with them will do a lot to determine where your path takes you. If you bump up against those obstacles, feel the resistance, and decide that it's impossible, then it will be so. Alternatively, if you hit a roadblock and view it as a sign to check in with your internal GPS and go into problem-solving mode, your potential is limitless. Let's take a look at some of the biggest roadblocks, barriers, and learning curves you may face on the road to achievement.

Hanging with the wrong crowd

Instead of helping you move forward, the people you choose to hang out with may hold you back. Recognize this type of roadblock. You may be encountering this roadblock if the people in your life constantly tell you that your dreams and ideas are crazy or way out there, or if they criticize your every move and don't celebrate your forward momentum.

This can lead to another serious roadblock, which is the danger of being pigeonholed. You need to surround yourself with what I like to call "passion partners." These are people who currently walk with you or want to partner with you in the pursuit of your passion.

Pigeonholed

This means to mentally classify someone into an oversimplified category based on certain factors. I experienced this mentality when I was trying to move into a revenue position and out of HR within the same company. Though I had a portfolio filled with high-performance skills, I was viewed as being limited to HR service delivery. I had to learn to use language that the revenue side of the business was accustomed to hearing and understand the particulars of that part of the business.

You may be painted into a particularly limiting role, especially if you are young and you come from an inner-city neighborhood or a single-parent home. People who are older or who have some level of life or work experience may perceive you as a "fixer-upper." They might see you as broken because your background is not the same as theirs. As a society, we don't know what is going on with people who are not like us. They may very well be making a big leap, assuming things about you that aren't true. Such invalid assumptions can seriously get in the way. It has made me more aware of being able to speak well too. I've had to learn how to articulate my transferable skills. It is an art form to share your vision with others in such a way that they can understand and connect with you.

Staying in your comfort zone

Depending on your definition of success, you will likely have to learn to do some things that are unfamiliar and, maybe, even uncomfortable at first. You'll know this has become a roadblock when you'd rather stay put than move into unfamiliar social circles, even if it means passing up a promotion. My advice: get past your comfort zone and diversify your learning.

Lacking confidence in yourself

What you think of yourself is often the biggest barrier of all. How you perceive your abilities and how you choose to act on your decisions can either impede your success or promote it. When you acknowledge your own progress, including the small steps and victories, you will grow in confidence. This confidence is one of the most important factors in achieving success in every area of your life.

Fear of losing your "street cred"

A significant personal barrier can occur when you start moving up the corporate ladder and you lose credibility on the street. Whenever I came back to visit the old neighborhood, there were always people who said, "Here comes the corporate guy visiting again!" Whatever. You have to let that go or reshape your view of it. Unfortunately, this attitude is pervasive in hip-hop culture: that it's not cool to speak well, pursue your education, or stand your ground. I call it "Mentaltraz"–as if you are permanently locked in a mental Alcatraz. When you succumb to this barrier, you are imprisoned. Make no mistake about it.

Falling for the seductive roadblock of success

It is so important not to gravitate toward the bright, shiny objects such as chasing money or titles. This is especially tough because the majority of people will think that this is the path you should be on. Some of the moves I have chosen to make in my career may not have looked so good from the outside (those lateral moves that were aligned with my overall development goals, but didn't have all of the perks, bells, and whistles). However, these were exactly what I needed at the time. Whenever I felt people challenging those decisions, I would ask myself, "Is this on my path, or am I being taken on a detour?"

Fear of learning curves

New learning possibilities are huge potential barriers if you allow other people's assessment of you or your own fears to interfere. Fear only becomes powerful when you give it your power. Instead of being afraid of facing the learning gap, focus on all the after-hours learning available. Be willing to take on extra learning after 5 p.m. After all, you can't learn everything on the job! Put in the hours to advance your skills and get rid of your fear of learning something new.

Losing control over your emotions

You can't always control what happens around you, but you *can* choose your reaction and how you handle your emotions in any situation. During team-building and leadership discussions, I often talk a lot about emotional intelligence and how important it is to maintain control over your feelings. What is the benefit of blowing up, anyway? I would rather assimilate what's going on and give a measured response. I prefer to mull over my options and digest what is being said. I have seen firsthand how difficult it can be to gain back credibility when you're perceived as a hothead or wear your emotions on your sleeve. When you step back and measure your emotions against your value set, you maintain power. If I choose my response, it is because I don't want to give you power over me.

This is powerful: I know my passion point. I know what I want to do. I know what I've set my GPS for. Having a direction and knowing where you want to go gives you freedom when you hit those learning curves or barriers. Consider the options against the journey planned so you can step away and think of it in your own terms, and figure out what to do.

Prepare, prepare, prepare

Preparation is the bedrock for shifting the perception of what you can or can't do.

My son has been playing football for quite a while now. He played Pop-Warner football in Philadelphia as a pre-teen. Once in high school, he played there as well with a view toward playing professionally. As he headed to college, he had hoped to get recruited by top football programs, but it didn't happen. Unfortunately, throughout my son's football experiences to date, he has experienced some of the same challenges I did, often coming close the pinnacle of success but not reaching it. In Pop Warner football, his teams did a good job but never won a championship. In high school, his team made it to the final playoffs and lost, taking them out of the championship run.

As a result, however, we worked to get him into a college football program. He selected key highlights from his high school football years, and I created a highlight reel. We uploaded that onto YouTube, prepared a form letter, and began reaching out to college football coaches. We created a spreadsheet to track it all and used a number of Websites to find the contact information for coaches and college recruiters. It was a lot of work, but we constantly prepared and, through it, he learned how to refine his pitch and get himself noticed.

He played for two years at Delaware State University before transferring to West Chester University. He still has an eye for moving forward and joining a professional football team; playing football is one of his passion points. All these twists and turns are another way to say that his course has not been a straightforward one so far. We've seen nothing that would say he is going to be recruited by NFL teams, his ultimate dream.

My advice to him, once again: prepare, prepare, prepare. Though the work here would be similar to what he did when he was coming out of high school, the expectations of the coaches and agents will be a little different. They will expect to see a young, independent man who knows what he wants and someone who can articulate why he deserves it.

I remind him, "You have to pitch yourself!" As he gets ready to call NFL agents to secure help in getting into tryouts, he will need to pitch and, in order to pitch, preparation is his greatest asset. I told him that his story couldn't simply be "I want to play." He needs a storyline that explains what he wants to do, why he wants to do it, how he has done it in the past, and why he believes he will be successful in the future. His pitch needs to be concise (90 seconds or less), and it must be compelling. He'll need to sell his abilities for today, but also show how he plans to parlay his NFL experience into the future.

No one likes to prepare. You just want to get to it! I understand that, but you have got to be buttoned up so that it sounds like you believe it. Once you have your general pitch done, you need to customize it for each individual conversation, acknowledging the person you're talking to. A key part of the preparation is researching the person you will be speaking with, understanding his or her background, history, who he's worked with, what made him successful, and so on. Just as you want others to understand who you are, you need to understand your audience too.

Re-program your GPS as needed

When I first went out to pursue a new opportunity within JPMorgan Chase, I went into conversations unprepared because I was known internally. As people within the organization reviewed my background, which was not on the revenue side of the business, they didn't feel I was a match. Without preparation, I was not able to make a compelling case. My story wasn't one that connected with them. At this early stage, I didn't have a clear story about my transferable skills that engendered their interest. With that learning experience, I went back and worked on the story/pitch. I was then better able to nail down definitively what I wanted and what I didn't want.

I realized that I needed to diversify my skills to go for this larger goal of reaching the level of CEO. When I solidified my desire to be in the C-Suite, I realized that I needed to work toward roles that would provide me with experience on the revenue side of the ledger. Up until that point, I had been primarily working in large human resources, operations, and services roles. Although they were complex and multi-site, and had large staffs and systems, they were on the expense side of the ledger and were essentially staff roles. I needed to get to the revenue side to hone those skills.

So I started on a journey to find a new job within the company. I scheduled appointments with key leaders across the company and, given my role then, I had access to different individuals, as they at least knew my name. The first few meetings were a little rough as, in hindsight, I didn't adequately prepare for them. I knew I wanted a new job on a revenue side of the company, but I hadn't narrowed down my priorities beyond that.

Nevertheless, it was a good learning experience as I also found that, though I was valued within the organization, I was regarded as an operations and services guy. After a few trips that certainly felt like they were not going to yield any opportunities for me, it was obvious that I needed to work on a few things. I needed to prepare, I needed to identify my key priorities, I needed to do a better job at projecting and selling my transferable skills, and I needed to be clear about what were non-starters such as doing things that I did not want to do. I constantly evaluated any new opportunities against my internal GPS. This kept me focused.

Without defining your vision, you will find it is almost impossible to reprogram your internal GPS. Without a vision, you have no idea where to start or even what the starting line looks like. Trust me, your GPS is working all the time and, left alone, it will take you to more of what you currently have. So how do you know when it's time to put in a new destination? Think of the things in your life right now that are bothering you; look at your situation from every point of view. Are you struggling with your personal relationships, with work, or with your health? Do you enjoy your hobbies? What causes you stress? Once you know the answers to these questions, you can reprogram your destination with the new coordinates—fill your internal GPS with the opposite of those things that are interfering with your happiness.

By staying in tune with your internal GPS, you can continually fine-tune the process. After realizing the importance of changing my approach to finding a new job, I had to go over those things that were important to me at the time. The first was that, as my son did not live with me, but was close by in the Philadelphia area, I wanted to make sure that I could see him regularly. The second thing was that I was looking for a revenue-oriented job, a role that would allow me to be a driver of revenue for the company on a clear basis. Armed with those priorities and a few others, I was more focused and ready to go back out into more exploratory discussions. It was a great learning experience, as I had a chance to meet a number of people.

Don't argue with your GPS

It was a great opportunity to leverage my transferrable skills while learning the business and driving revenue. However, there was some downside I had to strongly consider. I would lose a few things in this transition. First, status: I would go from being the HR service delivery executive for North America to one of many segment directors. Second, location: I moved from a corner office to a middle-of-the-floor office, from an executive administrative assistant to largely self service, from a large span of control of 200-plus people, 30-plus functions, and significant autonomy to an environment with reduced autonomy. And third, bonus compensation: though I would still be a senior vice president, it was a different group structure and thus a reduced bonus compensation target. Initially, this was all hard to swallow as I started to assimilate the changes. However, I felt like it was all an investment that would be well worth it over time, and my GPS said it would put me on the right road to my destination.

When you don't know what to do, do nothing. Get quiet so you can hear the still, small voice—your inner GPS guiding you to true North.

—Oprah Winfrey

A few years into the role, I wondered about that GPS from time to time. As with anything, there are changes that happen (such as team reductions, manager changes, team restructures, and strategy changes) that are beyond your control; your cheese gets moved. However, I found that my GPS was spot on. I learned and gained experiences that moved me further toward one of my passions.

Keep on the path

How are you going to get to *your* dreams without following your own path, even when it deviates from what looks, from the outside, like the "better" move? By reminding yourself that success on your own terms is just that: your own. It won't make sense to everybody else, and it doesn't have to. Here are some ways to ensure you are always in tune with your inner GPS:

- Remember that your brain is open to receiving coordinates for new destinations, but it is up to you to clearly define those destinations and work steadily toward making progress.

- When you come up against roadblocks or barriers, stay strong. The journey you have to take in life is uniquely yours. The paths you choose may look odd to others and defy conventional wisdom. However, you must stay focused on your goals.

- When it becomes necessary, reprogram your internal GPS. Stay in tune with your vision and, if you go off course (or the course you are on interferes with your happiness), then reprogram.

- Prepare for opportunities in advance by being clear about who you are, what you've accomplished, and where you are going.

7

Coaching Along the Way

• •

This chapter discusses the importance of leveraging "signs" along the journey to ensure you're still on the right road. Signs are in essence feedback and feedback is a gift, particularly when it comes from those vested in your success. This chapter provides some insights and techniques into how to keep the gifts coming. It includes ways to connect with a few mentors or coaches in order to help you move forward. We'll look at the different types of mentoring relationships that are available to you. We'll also discuss the importance of mentoring others and giving back no matter where you are on the journey.

Different types of coaching

Most people believe you need a formal relationship to get good coaching. I have found that there is a deep value to be found in developing and cultivating feedback from a wide variety of people. You can learn new ways to better yourself from many diverse coaching approaches. Let's take a closer look at some of the most common types of mentoring/coaching relationships:

- **Formal coaching.** Often, this is when you are involved with someone who is several levels above you in an organization or has a career in the same industry. This is a good relationship to develop when you seek valuable insight and want to understand how your mentor got to where he or she is today (and how you can get there too). A mentor within this context can potentially become a sponsor, someone who becomes an active advocate for you within the company, helping you to move up in your career.

- **Group mentoring.** These are relationships you create when you work on a team with an executive. This is when you develop relationships with leaders and gain invaluable experience by working alongside someone who introduces you to circumstances and situations that help you improve.

- **Peer-to-peer coaching.** This can be one of the richest types of coaching, as it comes from people with whom you work side by side. They can provide insights like no other, as long as you can take advice without becoming defensive.

- **Self-coaching.** In essence, this is what you are doing right now by reading this book. Self-coaching includes using any information channels available in order to help yourself.

Formal coaching: Is your antenna raised?

Choosing whom you ask to become a coach can be a skill all its own. I often looked for people who emulated skills and competencies that I believed would be areas of opportunity for me. Ed McGann did just that! Ed had been around JPMorgan Chase for quite some time, had worked with a number of CEOs and HR executives, and was the senior executive of compensation and benefits. I often wondered how he had attained such influence.

Given Ed's role and my continuous expansion of roles, I had good exposure to Ed. I eventually asked him to be a mentor and he agreed. During my trips to New York, I would try to catch up with Ed once a month or so. Eventually, I was promoted to HR service delivery executive for North America, taking on responsibilities for the HR Contact Center in Houston, Texas in addition to my previous responsibilities.

As I set out in my new role, I thought about opportunities to function differently and improve our performance. I would go out to the various HR executives for the lines of business; each line of business had a different HR executive. For example, the retail bank had an HR

> *Mentoring is a brain to pick, an ear to listen, and a push in the right direction.*
> —John Crosby

executive, the private bank had an HR executive, the investment bank had an HR executive, and credit card services had an HR executive. So I would attempt to get out to them to explain what we were doing, how we were doing it, and when things would come to fruition.

Things were going well over the course of a year; improvements were being made, we were performing better in many instances, and we were exceeding benchmarks within our various functions. However, when I would meet with Ed, he would seem less than congratulatory. During one of our meetings over the phone, Ed asked me a question that stopped me right in my tracks: "James, do you think your antennas are raised enough?" I wasn't sure what he meant at the time, so I asked for clarification. He then explained it was important for me to listen while I was meeting with all of these different departments. Talking and informing wasn't enough: I needed to hear what the HR executives had to say and, more importantly, what they weren't saying.

Although we had made a number of improvements, we hadn't done a great job of understanding the different needs of the businesses given the varied priorities of the HR executives and their constituents. Taking Ed's advice to heart, I met with everyone again. I dug deeper, spending more time with each HR executive and his or her team, listening, and examining the unique challenges that each of their businesses faced.

Throughout the process, I bounced different ideas of how to approach this with Ed, and he would provide some great insight. He often gave me things to think about relative to the different personalities, the geographic reach, the culture of the different businesses, and things to look out for. His counsel through this was invaluable and ultimately helped me drive through things with a line of sight and with eyes wide open to the challenges. I also learned what success looked like with alignment and a focused set of priorities that reflected the needs of each business.

Focus on getting things done

John Schmidlin was one of our CTOs (chief technology officers) during my time at JPMorgan Chase, with a great reputation for getting things done. Planning ahead for a trip to New York, I requested a meeting with John. Prior to that, I had only known of him through word of mouth, primarily through Jennifer Cavazzini (another mentor and manager at one point) and occasionally seeing him speak at a conference or two. I was impressed with his reputation.

Upon meeting John, he provided a warm welcome and then quickly shifted the conversation toward how my organization and I were performing. John had a simple motto: OTOBOS (on time, on budget, on scope). He guided our conversation toward these points, probing about my commitments to the organization and whether I was delivering on them. Though I felt somewhat under fire, I actually enjoyed that he pushed my thinking and "lens" in another direction, relative to my work. I knew in that first meeting that he would be a valuable mentor. During several months, I spoke to John a number of times, using him as a sounding board to talk about my initiatives and my progress toward them. I valued his insights related to prioritization and execution rigor, and, generally, his ability to get things done.

Group mentoring: the breakfast club

It occurred to me at one point that I gained a lot of wisdom through peer mentoring. Without knowing I was doing it, I often went to lunch with my peers, many of whom I would consider friends. During those lunches we would discuss the different challenges we were facing and how we intended to tackle them. So I decided to see if structuring something with my mentees, helping them engage in peer-to-peer mentoring, would be productive.

I assumed if I made a big deal out of it and called it a "meeting" that it might not be well attended. So I called it the breakfast club and let everyone know it was a time when I would be available for breakfast in the cafeteria every other Thursday. If they wanted to join me, they could, but there was no obligation. At the first meeting, eight people showed up and, after the introductions, I provided some ideas on how we could use the time together. I told those gathered that I thought it would be a benefit to share stories with each other. My hope was they would see that, once they shared their stories, they would then engage with each other and develop relationships that would help them deal with challenges. Each of these individuals was taking on some of the same challenges in unique and different ways.

Over the course of months, not only did the original people come back, they told others about it. The group continued to grow much to my delight as, for me, this was all about helping individuals learn to help each other. I would often say, "When you're waiting to get time to talk with me, you are walking past people who are dealing with the same things." I wanted them to realize that, if they leaned on each other, they could probably solve things faster. Sparks really flew once everyone got on board with the group mentoring.

Peer-to-peer coaching:
bonding over similar challenges

I have gained a lot of wisdom through peer mentoring and I highly enjoyed the relationships I had with my mentees. During my first six months at Chase Card Services, I developed about six new mentoring relationships, along with the six more from my previous role. More importantly, as I engaged in these relationships, the conversations tended to have a lot of common themes. Whether it was figuring out how to move to the next level, getting exposure, making lateral moves to gain experience, or perceptions of glass ceilings, the challenges were very similar. Thus, peer-to-peer coaching can provide one of the richest sources of insight, as you're able to get views from someone who may sit side-by-side with you, exchanging real-time observations and insights. Still, peer-to-peer feedback is often the most difficult type, as there are myriad dynamics you need to address.

Do not wait for leaders; do it alone, person to person.

—*Mother Teresa*

One of the reservations people have with peer-to-peer coaching is that you have to be willing to expose yourself to criticism. You have to be willing to ask for help and be confident enough about what you do so that constructive feedback helps mold you rather than break you down. It can also be hard to give honest feedback, as peers who value your relationship may be concerned about being critical and, potentially, damaging the relationship. There are also those who have a difficult time being objective and unbiased. So, though this type of coaching may be hard to establish at first, with time and trust, once you get clicking, it is worthwhile. You do yourself a disservice by setting up barriers and not being receptive to peer-to-peer feedback. You not only forego the chance to get feedback, but also to create an ally to help you act on it.

Find a thinking partner

During my tenure at JPMorgan Chase, I had the good fortune of developing a relationship with Randi Raskin Nash. Randi and I sat on the same management team in HR service delivery (HRSD). Through the years, as my role expanded and I eventually ran HRSD for North America, Randi and I, in addition to our teams, worked on a number of projects together. I gained an appreciation for her astute insights, project oversight, facilitation, and general management capabilities.

Randi quickly became a go-to person for me for a number of things. Although we never called it peer-to-peer coaching, we would often ask each other for feedback. We would exchange open, candid, and honest criticism with each other, always positive and constructive. I found that we would often push each other to dig deeper into certain areas, issues, or barriers, and challenge one another to think more broadly about options to resolve situations. It is great to have a thinking partner when you're working through a major decision and coming to a crossroads. Randi's background and openness have allowed her to play that role with me on a number of occasions. Randi left JPMorgan Chase a few years before I did, but our relationship has continued on, with our families getting to know each other as well. I highly value our relationship and look forward to it continuing into the years ahead.

Get under the surface

I like to teach members of my team the value of a skill I call "assimilating." What this looks like is this: I tell my team, "Here's what I'm sensing, feeling, or observing right now in this group." Then we talk it out with each other and as a team. When we talk out loud and share our thoughts, we can then move forward with assimilating—incorporating and integrating each other's ideas into a whole new picture. When I do this, I show them that you have to be willing to share your early, imperfect thoughts, and it requires a willingness to be transparent and show vulnerability. It helps to see what a work in progress really looks like. This inner "behind the curtain" view is crucial for people to see. Trends and pronouncements from a business leadership team don't just come out of nowhere. This gives my team practice in spotting what is going on underneath the surface.

Typically, we receive feedback at the official checkpoints. The truth is, though, that feedback is happening all along the way. When you pay attention and get under the surface, you can pull the diverse threads together for a more complete picture. Developing and reading feedback is a skill that, once mastered, will always help you grow. I strongly encourage you to invite and accept coaching from your peers.

Self-coaching: be there for yourself

Self-coaching is both the simplest and the hardest type of coaching. The simplicity of it is that you can coach yourself any time you need to. In fact, you are doing it right now by reading this book! This book is a tool for developing your self-coaching practices. Self-coaching can also be a challenge because we're not always good at seeing where we need to improve or how to motivate ourselves to change.

By developing the ability to self-coach, you will affect your future. You will gain knowledge that will influence your decisions. Self-coaching can be done in a variety of ways: through reading, listening to audiotapes, or downloading content onto your favorite digital device. Advice and empowerment are only a fingertip away in this digital age.

The essence of coaching: hone your feedback skills

Some of the most valuable skills you can learn from any successful mentoring relationship are the abilities to hone both your soft and hard skills. Learning and applying these skills will keep you moving forward no matter what happens or whatever your current situation looks like. Let's look at the difference between hard skills and soft skills, and how you can use both to get ahead in life. As with most skills, you can develop strategies or learn techniques to improve your abilities.

Hard skills

Years ago, these skills may have been lumped under technical or learned skills, those things that take years to master. These days, hard skills usually refer to those attributes that help you get things done, push people, and achieve bottom-line results. They are task-list oriented, focused on what to deliver, and putting it right in front of you. My mentor John was definitely a master of hard skills. His concern was always about "Is what you are doing on time, on budget, on scope? Are you nailing it?" And he always kept me aware of results. Hard skills are important and necessary in order to survive in any corporate climate.

Soft skills

Soft skills require thought, intuition, and more collaboration. These attributes can often be perceived as unnecessary or "touchy feely." Think of the difference between trying to "push it through" versus getting feedback and incorporating pieces of other people's ideas. I have found that people like to sense they have their fingerprints on something. So when I meet with my team and gauge their reactions, I try to incorporate that input into the decision-making process. The overall effect is more collaborative rather than just pushing my own agenda through. This was where my mentor Ed really excelled: he had a mastery of soft skills, such as self-awareness, emotional intelligence and the application of collective wisdom.

You can't lose with more insight

In order to truly develop benefit from coaching, you will need to access mentors across a variety of functions, departments, and even industries. Get counsel from different aspects of your organization, including newer employees who have a fresh view. Also, look for those people who can give you a taste of the legacy culture—those who've been around and have a more substantive understanding of the business. Seek out coaches with diverse temperaments and perspectives. The two mentors I've mentioned previously were very different. John held everyone to very high standards and he felt that excuses were not acceptable—just get it done. Ed knew everybody and knew how to network. He taught me the importance of thinking things through and controlling my reactions to any situation. Different temperaments give different perspectives, and the truth is I feel I can't lose with more insight gleaned from my various mentors' vast experiences.

You lose time if you go down the wrong road

When you go to people for counsel, it deepens your relationships with them. Asking for help shows that you are open to moving past transactional relationships to deeper, more engaged relationships. The input and trade-offs have been substantive for my having sought counsel along the way. It has, and still does, make the decision-making process smoother and more valuable. If you are headed down the wrong road and don't ask for guidance, you're losing time—and that's something you can't get back.

Life's most persistent and urgent question is "What are you doing for others?"
—Martin Luther King, Jr.

On the top of my office board is a phrase a colleague shared with me that stuck: "Are you working *in* the business or *on* the business?" When you are too focused working in the business, you are so in the depths that you can easily lose sight of the big picture. If you only look from the top and work on the business, then you can miss the details and nuances of a situation.

It's the same on your journey—both in your career and in your life. You have to adapt, and have the ability to look back and ask yourself, "Where am I on this journey?" Use your coaching and mentoring relationships to help keep perspective along the way. Also, reach out to those who are looking for a mentor. As I've shown, you'll have something of value to share with them no matter what stage of life you are in. Don't be afraid to be a mentor or coach for someone else. You never know what kind of difference you will make.

Feedback is a gift

As we've seen in this chapter, coaching is invaluable as you go along your journey in life. Coaching and mentoring provide feedback, which is a gift that comes from a wide variety of sources. We learned how to keep the gifts coming by connecting with mentors and coaches. Each type of coaching relationship adds value and can propel you forward. Diversity is an asset; seek out mentors from across the board, be they peers, executives, or CEOs. They can be within your organization or in a different industry altogether. Self-coaching will provide you with a lifetime of learning when you are willing to motivate yourself to dig deeper. The feedback gained from any mentoring relationship will hone both your hard and soft skills—each essential for your professional and personal development.

Along with getting a lifetime of advice, focus also on giving back. Reach out and help others along the way. You can mentor people and give back no matter what your circumstances or where you are on your journey. In summary, the best way to receive and give coaching is to:

- Assimilate a variety of feedback from different perspectives regularly. Many of my mentors had different skills and techniques that they passed along. It was my responsibility to take each of those lessons and apply them to my life. Make it a habit to gather feedback, and hone your ability to break it down and make it work for you. This needs to be done regularly.

- Develop a diverse network of go-to coaches and mentors in every kind of setting. I have learned as much from formal mentor/mentee relationships as I have from the more casual relationships with my peers and colleagues. The key is diversity.

- Be a sponge. Soak up coaching from as many channels as you can. I prefer to meet with people face-to-face and learn from others' experiences and situations. You may prefer to listen to audio books or attend seminars. The essential part is to be well informed in what you do by constantly seeking out more detailed information about your industry and key corporate initiative, and how they affect you.

- Actively seek out information. It's gold. The more you know, the better you can steer and direct. The worst thing is the misuse of time for lack of information; you just never get time back when you have to retrace your steps to get back on the right path. The best part is that information can come from anyone. Everyone you come in contact with has a story to tell and something to teach you. Be open to the stories that other people have to share. Story-telling is a valuable tool.

- Develop peer relationships for exchanging feedback in order to learn from each other so that you can grow both professionally and personally.

- Be there for yourself by developing your self-coaching skills, including using this book!

8

Promise 3: Promote With Purpose

● ●

When you think of promotion, what often comes to mind is the slick type of marketing that is so self-serving it's almost painful to watch. What I mean by promote with purpose is to recognize that there is real value in championing yourself in a way that is personal and persistent. There are some great rewards in life for those who stand confidently in their strengths and share their story authentically. Promoting with purpose also includes realizing how you can learn from other people's journeys. We will examine the act of working toward selflessness, which may seem counter-intuitive on such a personally driven journey. We will also look at how the different roles of those we meet and interact with on our journey affect us, and how we can be beneficial to each other.

Everyone has a story to share

As you go through your journey, you'll have the opportunity to meet countless people from all walks of life. One of the biggest mistakes I made in my earlier years was not paying more attention to the people around me. If you want to be a scientist, you tend to be focused on spending time with and learning from scientists. If you want to be a musician, you tend to spend time with and learn from other musicians. However, there is the potential to learn something interesting from every person around you. Here are just a few reasons why you should always tune in to those around you:

- Beyond the direct technical skills required for whatever you want to accomplish, there are a host of other skills needed that you can always sharpen by learning from others.

- People know people! As you share your interests with others, people tend to dig into their own network memory banks, and ideas "pop" in terms of what they have heard from others they know or who they might want to connect you to.

- Support, support, support. When you genuinely and appropriately share your story (meaning a dialogue, not just you talking endlessly), people will feel "let in" into a special place. This will become a passion point incubator. Honestly interacting and making a connection is something people usually don't take for granted. Furthermore, it's memorable. You'd be surprised how, when people come across something that they believe would be helpful, they will pass it on to you.

- It's all about learning. There are many ways to learn, of course: reading, listening to radio, watching TV, and so on. I find interactive learning to be the best for me.

A learning experience on wheels

Some of the learning interactions I value the most are my dealings with drivers–whether it is a car service or taxicab. Often, people just provide the driver with directions or, if heading to a new place for the first time, they might inquire about the area. However, I have found that this is a great time to get to know a person a little and hear about his or her journey.

When I was leading HR service delivery for North America at JPMorgan Chase, I would try to visit HR in Houston about once a month. I would get a black car service and, fortunately, they would use a gentleman named BJ fairly consistently. Through time I got to know BJ, about his family, and his journey from being a driver to owning his own service. Through his story, I heard about some of the choices he made and how he arrived at a driving career versus doing other things that would have been more exciting for him, economically. I learned how he came to own his own company, the risks he took, and how he approached life. Anytime I had the opportunity to ride with BJ, I could count on it being a learning experience on wheels!

Everyone has something to teach you

Just as everyone has a story, almost everyone has something to teach you. Some lessons serve as cautionary tales, making you think, "I sure don't want to do that," whereas others hold a lifetime of wisdom and experience. These stories come from people who walk by you every day; you just have to be interested in their lives to learn from them.

In my day-to-day environment, I have the opportunity to speak with a few of the cleaning ladies some evenings and learn about the latest news from their families. They share with me how they're dealing with

> *Wisdom is the reward you get for a lifetime of listening when you'd have preferred to talk.*
> —Doug Larson

the challenges presented by their children—whether it's someone heading off to college, dealing with the latest boyfriend or girl-friend, and even updates on those who are in college.

You may be asking, "How do these things help me?" First, one of my passions is just helping people, so if there is anything I can offer from my experiences or from my current professional seat, I am more than happy to do so. Second, my journey still has a lot of road ahead, so these stories often give me something to deposit into my "wisdom bank," which I know I will draw on in the future. Third, I am in a consumer-oriented business (as many of us are). This is a chance to hear what is on the consumer's mind—not just the questions I ask in market research—but what is really going on in the life of a consumer and how I might meet their needs or the considerations I should have when trying to introduce my organization's product or service.

Interestingly, what I used to do by accident, I now do on purpose. I have gravitated toward spending more time with people, observing, listening, and engaging. I am more appreciative of the learning outcomes and the opportunity for it to be a "wisdom exchange."

Create a wisdom exchange

One of the most difficult things for me to achieve was being open to telling my story. I find that people are usually of two extremes: they're either too boastful or they don't share at all. I finally learned that telling your story for the benefit of others is not a form of self-aggrandizement; it is an opportunity for an exchange. Once I figured out it was okay to share my dreams, my passion, and my journey, I learned valuable lessons about where I've been and where I'm headed. I've discovered that my willingness to share often helps others get comfortable with doing the same.

The greatest good you can do for another is not just to share your riches but to reveal to him his own.

—Benjamin Disraeli

I wasn't always this open to dialogue. Earlier in my career, whenever I was in a situation and took a personality-type test such as Myers-Briggs, I used to test as an extreme introvert, but over the last decade, I have moved into the extrovert zone. I attribute this to the exchanges I've experienced and the various roles I've held. In 2008, I had an opportunity to spend some quality time with Jamie Dimon, chairman and CEO for JPMorgan Chase. On a whim, I sent him an e-mail, outlining my admiration of his career and his journey. I included a soft request to meet with him one day, if time would allow. He made it happen. Upon arriving at his office that day, I was ushered to a waiting room and told that he would arrive in 15 minutes and that I would have about 15 minutes with him. Of course, I sat there, thinking about the best way to use that time to gain some perspective from him on a few key things.

To my surprise, he simply walked in and flopped into the chair and said, "Hey, James. Good to finally meet you." It totally caught me off guard. As I tried to launch into my story, he wasn't having any of it. Instead, he asked me about my family—how I met my wife, how my family was, and what they were doing. He told me about his family and how important family time was. We eventually talked about work, but it was less about JPMorgan Chase and our successes, and more about what he learned when he failed, such as when he was fired from Citibank, and how he stayed motivated during that time in order to get himself back in the game (boxing helped). This was undoubtedly one of the best "wisdom exchanges" I've ever had. Our 15-minute conversation turned into 40 minutes, and gave me a totally different perspective on a person than I had prior to that conversation.

Ask insightful questions

Another aspect of promoting with purpose is that it provides you with the context to ask questions. For example, once I knew I wanted to be a CEO, I created a short list of folks I wanted to meet, each of whom I believed I could learn something from. The list originally included people such as Russell Simmons (of Def Jam and Phat Farm) and Clarence Otis, Jr. (CEO of Darden Restaurants). The list has grown through time and I haven't met most of the people I originally added to the list. However, creating the list prompted me to craft my story in case I got the chance to share it. I wanted to know what to tell them and what I would ask if I got 15 minutes of time with them. My list included people whose stories I wanted to hear so I could get a 360-degree view of the person. I didn't just want the headlines; I wanted to know about the pivotal moments of their lives. I wanted to learn about the challenges and failures too. I encourage you to make your own list of people you want to interview and what questions you would ask. Also, think about your own story and how that factors in. Here are some keys to creating an insightful exchange that allows you to self-promote, without making it all about you:

- Be authentic and genuine.
- Be curious. Have an intellectual curiosity.
- Find value in others and in their experiences. Seek out those people who you feel you can benefit from. When you do, they in turn find value in you, your experiences, and story.
- Remember that this is an exchange.
- Ask questions about the job they do: How did you get into this business? Do you still like it? What did you do to become successful?

If there is any one secret of success, it lies in the ability to get the other person's point of view and see things from that person's angle as well as from your own.

—Henry Ford

Creating a list of questions gives you a vision of what is possible and allows you to see how many different approaches there can be to get to similar places. To hear a person's story is very engaging and a great way to get to know someone. The backstory, the under-story, will give you the inside view on how that public success came about. These stories are a way to find points of relevance and learn from them. There are hard and easy ways to learn. One of the phrases I always remember is this: experience is the best teacher, but wisdom is to learn from someone else's experience.

Have a point of view

When you ask questions, have a point of view and be ready to share it. For example, have you been able to have a family and balanced lifestyle? What has gone into making you who you are, and what experiences and exposures bring you to this moment? If you are a young person, you are likely to find yourself being dismissed as someone no one wants to learn from. Please recognize that age alone does not necessarily buy you wisdom. I have learned everything I know about Instagram from my 9-year-old niece. And my son has introduced me to the Vine, which is a short, funny, and instructional video clip Website. I'm learning from young people every day!

When I take on new roles and new teams, I ask myself, "Who else is involved in this body of work? Who else has a different perspective? How can I get diverse perspectives without trial and error or without making assumptions?" The answers can be found in talking to people, asking insightful questions, and listening to their replies.

How do you process other people's wisdom? We all have filters; we're always seeking "credibility." Often, we discount people too quickly. We want to hear the success stories and tend to avoid the stories of those who look like failures. Both are equally valuable—there's a story behind the guy on the street. "God does not manufacture losers." People get into situations because of choices, situations, and barriers. There's a story behind that, too, and it can be beneficial to you. All you have to do is learn how to gather the wisdom from the story.

Let your whole self show

Several months ago, as I was bouncing through the halls at Allstate, a colleague yelled out: "Hey, Trig." This caught me off guard, as Trig is my nickname within the music industry. He then went on to tell me that when he noticed my profile and the youth-oriented work I do with Holy Culture (*www.holyculture.net*) and

Corelink Radio (*www.corelinkradio.com*), he took a look at the Websites to get a better idea of what it was all about.

During his investigation, he found out more about what I did in relation to youth and Christian culture. When he discovered that all of these people call me "Trig," it tickled him a bit. He said, "All of these people and kids just interact and call you that and they have no idea of your significance in a company like Allstate." I told him that when engaging with people, particularly youth in many cases, my title and accolades are not important; in fact, they could be prohibitive. When you are promoting with purpose, it is essential to have transparent conversations with no pretense. Through the years, I have had the opportunity to informally share with and mentor a number of artists and record label owners; sharing business practices to help them get better at what they do. Conversely, I learn a lot from them, particularly those that spend more time trying to operate within the music industry.

Because God gave you your makeup and superintended every moment of your past, including all the hardship, pain, and struggles, He wants to use your words in a unique manner. No one else can speak through your vocal cords, and, equally important, no one else has your story.

—Charles R. Swindoll

So, though I don't hide what I do, I don't lead with it. I work on building relationships and promoting the relevant things I do with people based on the interactions we are having. Years ago, I used to strive to keep things separate. During the past few years, however, I have become more comfortable with letting my whole self show. My sense is that increased confidence just came from experience, and the realization that I need to be "me" 100 percent of the time and share myself in that exact way. Later, in discussing how to develop your network or platform, I will share some of the best practices that have worked for me in bridging this seeming divide via social media.

Promoting with purpose is necessary in order to experience a whole-hearted embrace of your passion. When you promote with purpose, you deliberately reach out to others to share your story, make a connection, and listen to their stories. It is through making connections with others that you can learn from their experiences and apply those lessons to your own life. In summary, the best way to promote with purpose is to remember:

- Everyone has something to contribute, so be curious with people. Get to know those around you, and be open to making conversation and sharing stories. People sometimes discredit others as not being useful, but the truth is that there's something to learn from everyone.

- Stories open doors of connection and engagement. Practice your story by making a list of influential people you would like to interview—the sky is the limit. Pick anyone you can think of whose journey might be helpful to learn more about. When you make your list, choose those who have a relevant connection to what you are trying to do or whose experiences will resonate with you. Write out your questions and think of how your story connects with theirs. This story-telling will act as a kind of "wisdom exchange."

- Promoting with purpose starts by knowing your point of view. Knowing where you stand and being clear on how you got where you are will allow you to process other people's wisdom. Once you have a point of view, all you have to do is learn how to gather the wisdom from the stories that are shared with you. It will change every aspect of your life.

9

Networking: A Second Job

• •

This chapter discusses how to build, maintain, and leverage a network in a natural way. Networking can often feel like a burden, a task, or nuisance. However, if approached appropriately, it can become very natural, fluid, and rewarding, particularly as you connect with those on a similar journey. Some of the techniques shared here will debunk concerns and help you simplify the effort.

In Chapter 6, I discussed the story of how I moved from the support side of the banking business, albeit from a senior-level position, to the business-generating side of the business. Networking within the organization and relentless information interviewing were how I moved forward to the other side of the business, when others told me it could not be done.

Networking is a crucial link

People often shrug off the importance of networking, questioning its value under the guise of "my work should speak for itself." However, this is just not true. Melissa Giovagnoli says it very well in her book *Networlding: Building Relationships and Opportunities for Success*:

As teenagers—whether you are currently in high school, starting your college careers, or looking for your first job—you are in a position to start laying the foundation for your life in the adult world. Now is really the time to start thinking about making connections with the people who are going to help you both now and in the future. Life is all about building meaningful connections, and the more of these you have now, the easier it will be for you to fulfill your dreams and live the life you have always imagined. Having a great education is only part of the process. The people you meet now—in school, on your sports teams and your extra-curricular activities, in your places of worship—are the ones who are going to open doors for you in the future in ways that you may not even imagine.

It takes 20 years to build a reputation and five minutes to ruin it. If you think about that, you'll do things differently.

—Warren Buffett

In your plan to promote yourself with purpose, networking is a crucial link. In the movie *War Games*, the computer was all seeing and all knowing, able to assimilate information from everywhere. Although the all-knowing computer may seem intimidating or scary, it's actually an image of what you do when you're "on" your networking game. With technology on your side, a lot of what you are dealing with are information and access to information. In this day and age, that is incredibly powerful.

Networking gives you a crazy web to connect to a diverse world of information and people. People are connected to people, and people are constantly learning. Thus, networking is your opportunity to bring all of that to you. You can Google it, learn via Wikipedia, or talk to people within your own network, connecting with their personal experiences.

Build a network

You can start a network with just one other person. The key is to start wherever you are. Use the time you have wisely. I have found one of the most effective ways to make good use of my time and network simultaneously is during breakfast and lunch. My personal motto is "Never eat alone!" Let's assume that, minus vacations, holidays, and business travel, we have 40 clear work weeks a year to apply this method—that is, 10 opportunities a week or, minimally, 400 per year building and nurturing my network.

It is healthy to get away from your desk and eat lunch with someone you want to get to know better. Reach out, and find a point of commonality or something that intrigues you and makes you want to learn more. When you make yourself available on a regular basis, you'll find you can get that one-on-one with the expert in order to go deeper into a topic, issue, or conversation. You can stretch yourself across different departments, learning what other people in other parts of the company are involved in. Or you can use this time to connect with members of your own team or department. For example, I regularly have breakfast and lunch with key peers. Bosses, peers, and direct reports are all part of your network. You can have transactional relationships or you can go deeper; it's up to you. Know their personal side and get to know them more deeply so that the exchanges can become richer.

Networking is not about just connecting people. It's about connecting people with people, people with ideas, and people with opportunities.
—Michele Jennae

Take advantage of your company's assorted internal meetings that are set up for special interests. These fly past us when our days are busy, yet they are a golden opportunity to connect with your colleagues, peers, and collaborators, as well as guest speakers. These meetings, including encounters such as a "lunch-and-learn," are designed to be networking-friendly sessions within your corporations. These events are set up for the purpose of getting to know your peers and team members—that is, networking.

Given all the technological advances, it can be harder to make the commitment to show up in person. I don't know if you will ever replace the power of meeting someone face-to-face, to share a handshake and see unspoken body language (which often say more than the words), for establishing a connection with another person. Electronic communication is wonderful and though I appreciate its convenience, for the most part I prefer to meet in person. That is a gift of mine; as a people person, I like to connect in person to engage more deeply with others. I find that there are benefits to meeting face-to-face and make it happen whenever possible. According to research from a recent national survey of corporate and association meeting planners with the Convention Industry Council, "Face-to-face meetings build trust and relationships; live meetings result in more effective exchange of ideas and face-to-face meetings provide the human connection that powers business" (*Face Time. It Matters.* ConventionIndustry.org).

Network to your next job

According to a report from ABC News, 80 percent of today's jobs are found through networking. These are people who understand the importance of building personal connections, so they start the process of creating a network and keep it going, even after they have a job. If you share your story, people will think of you when relevant resources, information, and people come through their field.

From a job-seeking perspective, it's what helps get your resume to the top of the pile. When I connect with younger members on my team, they frequently say they are applying for some posted position within the organization. Too often, they tell me they are putting the application in "the system." I ask them, "Do you know the hiring manager? Do you know the HR recruiter?" Usually they say no. They are counting on a faceless piece of paper that pops up in the system to tell their story. How effective do you think that is? The cold, hard fact is that employees who are known in some way to their future employer are perceived as being better hires.

So I keep at them. "Who do you know who knows the hiring manager? Is there someone within your circle who can speak up for you and your abilities? Do you know someone who would be willing to say, 'Here's why I'd like to have him on my team'?" You need an advocate who has seen you fail and find the gumption to get back up, someone who will speak well of you. I follow the same process for internal positions too. When I get a call from a person I trust in my network, it's gold when he or she recommends someone who would be a perfect fit for a position. For a hiring manager, slashing the time to fill a position from 80–100 days down to 10–15 is gold. The result is that people come to me almost every day with folks they recommend.

People sometimes don't like it when I talk about networking and personal connections; it makes them uncomfortable. But the truth is, when you are planning your strategy and breaking through the bubble,

> *If you are the only one who can speak on your behalf, you are probably in trouble.*
> —James Rosseau

you think in simple terms. After all, when you play a pickup game of hoops, to whom do you gravitate and pick if you are the team captain? You pick people you are comfortable with, those you know and feel you can work with. Networking, especially around the hiring process, is much the same. You can call it politics, but networking is important to developing your influence. You need to exercise and develop it like a muscle, because it will always be a benefit to build and maintain a healthy network.

One of the things I found was that, whenever you meet people, they will typically give you two or three other people they believe that you should meet. When I moved from the support side of the banking business to the business-generating side, I had an opportunity to spend time with some people in the treasury services and solutions business. Heidi Miller was the CEO at the time. She spent some time talking to me and, during our conversation, referred me to Mo Osborne, who was the chief operating officer for Treasury and Securities Services (TSS). As we spoke, Heidi picked up the phone, called Mo, and asked her if she could meet with me. Mo obliged and there I went, jogging down to her office. Mo gave me a warm welcome, walked me through her organization, which was huge, with a number of COO and CTO opportunities across the globe. She naturally referred me to a number of individuals whom I met with, and within several weeks, I was offered a CTO job in South Africa! Unfortunately, though that would have been a huge step up in my career, it was not aligned with my priorities at the time, so I was unable to pursue that position. However, the point is that, absent the proactive networking, I don't believe the opportunity would have even surfaced. I would not have known the position was available, nor would anyone have probably brought it to my attention, as they would not have known I had an interest.

Maintain your network

Not everyone will fall into the same category within your network. With some contacts, you will maintain a deep connection; with others, it will remain more business like. You will know a lot of people, and some will become friends. With others, you will enjoy an acquaintance type of relationship, such as on social media like Facebook and LinkedIn. I look for quality and depth over volume. When you connect, be sure to have a great exchange. When you are feeling enlightened and refreshed after meeting someone, those are the contacts you want to maintain. Consciously create standing appointments. Meet regularly for breakfast, for example. Figure out how frequently you want to meet with people. Set up standing meetings with certain people: quarterly, monthly, and annually.

Whenever I find myself involved in a series of network-friendly web of meetings, I utilize my project management skills. I have learned to track all of my meetings, activity, and takeaways to ensure I follow up with people promptly and send thank-you notes. Keeping your network organized and within reach is key! Here are some tips on getting and staying organized:

It isn't just what you know, and it isn't just who you know. It's actually who you know, who knows you, and what you do for a living.
—Bob Burg

- Follow up with any promised contacts right away.

- Keep track of what you promised and what additional steps are required.

- Make note of what you did. How did networking serve you in the situation?

- What did you learn from this networking interaction?

- Create a spreadsheet of the people you've contacted and how you've maintained contact with each person. This will give you a quick file to review and a convenient way to have your information in one place.

The next page has an illustrated example of this last point.

Name	Referral Source	Title	Business / Company	Contact Info	Meeting Date	Notes	Status
Heidi Miller	N/A	CEO	JPMC TSS	XXX-XXX-XXXX XXX@jpmchase.com	6/1/05	- Initial Meeting: Heidi believes it is important for me to meet with Mo Osborne and Melissa Moore. - 6/3/05: Thank-you note sent to Heidi. - 6/11/05: Follow-up note sent to Heidi providing her with short debriefs from meetings with Mo and Melissa.	Closed
Mo Osborne	Heidi Miller	COO	JPMC TSS	XXX-XXX-XXXX XXX@jpmchase.com	6/1/05	- Mo has a number of regional CTO/COO roles and would like me to meet with David Ham and Monty Illabus. - 6/5/05: Thank you note sent to Mo. - 6/14/05: Follow- up note sent to Mo, debriefing meetings she recommended.	Open
Melissa Moore	Heidi Miller	President	JPMC Treasury Services	XXX-XXX-XXXX XXX@jpmchase.com	6/10/05	- Initial Meeting: Melissa did not have any opportunities at the moment, but asked that I follow up with her in a few months (tickler placed on calendar for 9/1/05).	Open
David Ham	Mo Osborne	COO - EMEA	JPMC TSS	XXX-XXX-XXXX XXX@jpmchase.com	6/12/05	- Initial Meeting: Believes there are several opportunities that may be a fit. David promised to follow up with me in 2–3 weeks (tickler set on calendar for 7/1/05). - 6/13/05: Thank-you note send to David.	Open
Monty Illabus	Mo Osborne	COO - Americas	JPMC TSS	XXX-XXX-XXXX XXX@jpmchase.com	6/13/05	- Initial Meeting: Opportunities are limited at this time and do not appear to be a fit. - 6/14/05: Thank-you note sent to Monty.	Closed

How to leverage a network

Remember that networking is not about collecting contacts; it's about making connections, building ties, and ultimately doing business. To leverage your network effectively, you'll need to:

- Make your network your "go to" for whatever you are looking for. If you have a need for something, ask someone in your network first. For example, if you need a plumber, ask people in your network. They will tend to provide you with someone they've had personal experience with and can therefore recommend. This is due to a feeling of accountability for overall outcomes.

- Share your passion, goals, and aspirations. People in your network are often interested and even excited to know what drives you. You'll be amazed at how much they retain and how they can be great, proactive advocates for you.

- Activate through your network. For example, as I was in the process of writing this book, I reached out to a number of folks in my network for thoughts on how to promote it. I searched for people who worked in human resources, or had access to influential media personalities that could provide a perspective on how to approach the process.

When networking works proactively for you, it's a real give and take. Once you begin interacting with people, they will know your interest and your story, where and what you've come from, and they will know your passion. When something comes up that sounds close to what you are about, they can make introductions to others who are "right up your alley." In this way, networking becomes intensely helpful and powerful.

Networking expands your base of influence and your resources

When I was leaving JPMorgan Chase for my new role at Allstate in Chicago, several people in my network offered to help me make some personal connections there. Monica Hawkins helped make a key connection. I spoke to her by phone once I got on the ground in Chicago; she said, "I could point you to a dozen people, but I want to make it easy. I will point you to just one person who can help." Indeed, that was true. She connected me with Billy Dexter, who in turn has introduced me to at least 12 amazing people. When I had a recent need for a patent attorney, I turned to Billy for a recommendation. I would always rather go with people I know and feel comfortable with, so if they're connected to Billy, they're in. When I put my network to good use, it is like having my own personal Angie's List!

> *The currency of real networking is not greed but generosity.*
> *—Keith Ferrazzi*

When I began sharing stories with Billy about my challenges growing up in Philadelphia, he shared his issues with growing up in Detroit. It was during that conversation that I disclosed that I would someday like to turn my stories and experiences into a book. His response was, "Hey, before you go forward, you should flesh out your idea more. I can get you in touch with a book coach who can help you move through the process." I met with the book coach, Melissa, and she helped me put my thoughts into the contents of this book. On her recommendation, I located an agent and a publisher too. Had I not met Monica, I would not have met Billy. Had I not met Billy, I would not have met Melissa. And this book you're reading right now may never have happened!

A mutually beneficial exchange of opportunities

Often, the thought of networking can seem overwhelming, especially if you are just starting out and aren't sure how to effectively make connections. If you are introverted or unaccustomed to building bridges, networking can feel like an impossible burden. However, if approached consistently and with the right approach, it can be a very rewarding process. Some of the techniques we discussed in building, maintaining, and leveraging a healthy network include the following:

- Networking begins with you. It can start with one name: yours. You are the one who needs to take the first step to open yourself up to creating an active, fluid, living and breathing network that you can count on.

- Networking that works is really a one-to-one, mutually beneficial exchange of opportunities. If you are overwhelmed with an image of a vast network of people surrounding you, remember that each point of contact is a person—a fellow human being. Each connection is just like having a friend, one who helps you out and someone you like to help, as well.

- Start with a few connections and build them up over time. It's easy to confuse activity with accomplishment when you are first trying to develop something from nothing. Resist the urge to add everyone you meet to your contact list. Instead, be selective and focus on building strong connections that can build exchanges.

- Be proactive and reach out to those important connections, your "first string," and nurture the relationships on a regular basis. This would include calling, e-mailing, and meeting in person at least once a month. Keep track of your strongest (and potentially strongest) connections so that you can take advantage of any opportunities you see for yourself or on their behalf.

- It's paramount that you follow through on any promises you make. You want to be someone others can rely on to get things done. This is where organization plays a key role. Take notes after each connection you make to keep track of any obligations you may have committed to. Stick with it; persistence and perseverance count.

- Develop your network so that you can always go to them first. As I've stated, my network often feels like I have my own Angie's List.

10

Propelling Your Power

• •

People like to be associated with success; like it or not, it's human behavior. One of the quickest and most effective measurements of success can be found in strong proof points. Proof points are also called evidence. Just as evidence is required in a court of law to prove a point, establishing strong proof points is the key to giving you credibility and validating your claims. These are claims pertaining to your performance, your abilities, and your achievements. The more evidence you have, the more believable your claims.

How can you develop proof points and create a broad definition of success? As a society, we often have a bias to see success as the home run. Success for many is the Grammy award–winning artist. It's winning the Super Bowl, the NBA championship, or the World Series. It's being the popular champion on a show like *American Idol, The Voice,* or X *Factor.* The problem with this mentality is that we often fail to recognize the value of the *singles.* Imagine that you couldn't hit the ball yesterday but today, when you went to hit the ball, you made contact and reached first base. Now, this single may not represent success to the world at large, but to you this is progress!

Facts are stubborn things, and whatever may be our wishes, our inclinations, or the dictates of our passions, they cannot alter the state of facts and evidence.

−John Adams

It is essential to define success along your journey, both for yourself and for others. I advocate using proof points or the small wins that you make along the way. There is one recent single that comes to mind. When I joined Allstate in the fall of 2011, I entered with a vision of creating differentiation with our Affinity business. Our tagline as a team became "changing the way people think about insurance." A few of us had experience with offering consumers rewards for their purchases, and we wanted to try it in insurance. We had seen great things happen in other industries and early testing we did with a potential partner showed the same might be true for insurance.

However, we were counseled by several people that rewards didn't exist in the insurance industry due to regulations that prohibited "rebating." It was thought that giving consumers anything that might be considered a reward for purchasing insurance would not be allowed. Still, over several months, we established a team of folks from a number of departments and introduced rewards in the industry. We were successful at getting a number of states to approve our approach and launched our first rewards offering with United Mileage Plus in March of 2013—a huge single!

Once you can discuss your proof points, the next step is sharing your journey with others and talking about how you have gone from small wins to even bigger victories. This gives others a way to reframe how they see their own success even as it helps them engage in your journey. This second point is important as the more people who champion you on your journey, the more supportive your network, and the better your sustainable success.

Another vital aspect of sharing your proof points is that different types of people relate to or respond to different types of proof points. It is a good idea to have a variety of proof points to choose from when you are sharing important messages. That way you can pick and choose different kinds of proof points to target various people. Here is how I use proof points to engage with others and create momentum. I'll begin with my story of how I created an e-mail "Thought of the Day" message to inspire and motivate the people in my department and how it grew to have a life of its own.

Propelling others with the "Thought of the Day"

When I joined JPMorgan Chase in 2000, we had a team of about 60 on the Payroll Services team. Although I tried to walk the floor regularly to interact with everyone, the flurry of meetings and other things often made that a challenge. In addition, our physical environment was one of high cube walls, which separated everyone into their own little worlds. Back then, we did not have a meeting room large enough to accommodate crowds, even if we did want to do an all-hands meeting. It was during this time that I began what I called the "Thought of the Day."

What is the thought of the day? It is something I started doing back in February of 2000. I had gotten into the habit of sharing things with my team such as my thoughts on key topics, our current situation, and our future outlook. During my morning commute from Philadelphia to New

> *The reason we struggle with insecurity is because we compare our behind-the-scenes with everyone else's highlight reel.*
> *—Steven Furtick*

York, I would read the newspaper or other materials, and I would often find a noteworthy thought or quote that would resonate with me. These were simple yet profound messages that stayed in my mind as I went through my daily commute. I decided to share these things with my team during our morning meetings when I would open with something I'd read or heard.

I chose items that I considered inspirational or thought provoking. I wanted to give everyone a chance to pause and reflect, to consider the relevancy of this information for the day ahead. Trust me, it wasn't too deep. I loved to read something motivational on my way to work and it was also an opportunity to ensure everyone heard from me every day. I always made sure the Thought of the Day contained ideas that I genuinely felt or was moved by.

I decided to share these messages through e-mail each morning. When I started doing this, I didn't expect it to go on for long, but it soon became part of my morning routine. Through time, I found that these e-mails became a part of other people's routine too. At first, the response from others was often a simple, "Hmmm, that's interesting" or "Thanks for sharing that." As time went on, though, it became a daily expectation. If I forgot to send one in the morning, I could count on someone somewhere coming up to me in the hallways and asking, "Hey, what happened to the Thought of the Day? I missed it this morning!"

After the Chase and JPMorgan merger and our subsequent move, I was responsible for managing a larger group and, with each change within the organization, I remained consistent in sending out my daily messages. As we progressed, I sensed that people were feeling extremely challenged in their respective roles given the amount of work, abbreviated time frames, and tremendous amount of change going on. The Thought of the Day continued being popular partly because it offered people something light, a word or two that would help them cope with all of the challenges we were dealing with.

Through time, as the team grew to more than a few hundred, I would often get responses back from people with a follow-up thought or question. The next thing I knew, people who were not part of my organization would request to be added to the Thought of the Day e-mail list. Back then, I didn't have such a list, so I quickly created one, and it continued to grow for quite some time. As we had people in other cities that I only saw about once a month, this was an excellent way to maintain some personal contact with them as well. Many times when I visited these other cities, as I walked through the various areas of the organization, people would often greet me; it felt like they knew and were comfortable with me. This was partly because they heard from me every day and it was not just a business update; it was personal. These Thoughts of the Day spoke to the core of who I was and what I was feeling. By sharing the thoughts that resonated with me, I was able to reach out and touch people in an engaging way.

Since then, I have gone through different roles, but there has always been at least one constant: sending the Thought of the Day. Through time, as people have shared this with others, I have had many ask to be added to the distribution list. Now the list includes people not only from my organization, but from across many different platforms. I invite you to join the list as well. Please go to *www.jamesrosseausr.com* and click on "Thought of the Day" if you would like to be included on the distribution list.

Start your day with purpose

As I stated, one of the reasons I began the Thought of the Day concept was because the morning is that time of day when I get inspired and I wanted to motivate others as well. I've come to realize how important it is to think about how you start your day and where it puts you mentally as you dive into your work.

Let me ask you: How do you feel when you wake up every morning? Do you begin the day sluggish and tired, or are you—for the most part— energized and excited about the pos-

The first hour of the morning is the rudder of the day.
—Henry Ward Beecher

sibilities ahead? Your attitude at the start of the day can have more effect on you than 10 cups of coffee!

When you begin each day focused, the vision you have for your life will become clearer, real, and achievable. When your mornings begin with focus, you understand better the value that each passing minute gives you. Whether you like to begin your day with a big breakfast or a run, I would challenge you to test various routines and monitor how well they start you off. Does your routine let you get the most out of your time? I have found a routine that works well for me. Most of my days begin with prayer, working out, my favorite coffee, a light breakfast, and sending out the Thought of the Day.

By sharing the words and thoughts that motivate me, I not only connect with others, but also share my personal story with a larger audience. Success stories motivate people; they also provide you with an opportunity to get your story out. In addition, sharing your story gives you the chance to keep your network growing, as more people will begin to share it on your behalf. A successful story, however, requires that you tell a *great* story in a compelling and engaging way. Here are some tips and techniques that will help you create your own captivating and appealing narrative.

Tell a great story

One of the keys to a great story is that it usually involves someone else as the hero or heroine rather than yourself. The focus is on how that person overcame some significant hardship and how you learned from that experience. Through narrative, you offer the reader or listener the process by which you learned so that others can use the same to address similar hardships.

Another aspect is to remember that everybody has a different way of thinking about story-telling. I feel most comfortable talking about other people and sharing what I've learned from them. You may want to focus on a theme that contains a center point for your story. This enables your audience to learn from the story and not get confused with too many points. I usually have a central point that I will open and close with, and then offer three or four supporting points. I follow up with relevant facts. Next, I share a story that will support the points.

As mentioned, various audiences respond to different types of stories. Be open to developing a few that capture different elements. The story I use most often—and tweak frequently, depending on my audience—is the one about the platinum hand-cuffs (discussed in Chapter 3). It is perfect for people early in their career as it helps them think about how they will navigate their journey and whether or not they have inadvertently given up some of themselves for the sake of material rewards. My stories are always where I share my journey. But before I jump into one of my proof points, I identify how it is connected to my journey and think about my target audience. For example, recently I have been going through a job change. When I share this with others, I let them know that, although I can't always anticipate everything, what often comes my way always seems to be relevant to my journey. In other words, I believe in serendipity.

The inward look

Serendipity is defined as "the occurrence and development of events by chance in a happy or beneficial way." To me, serendipity is also about creating space for opportunity. As I shared in the last chapter on building networks, in order to consistently build your string, you have to allow for chance. Creating serendipity is about allowing things that would be beneficial for you and your career to organically emerge. When you add people into your life, what looks like one conversation with one person, can turn into an opportunity of a lifetime. If you allow your conversations to flow more freely, you create a space of possibility. Little did I know when I began a conversation with Don Fleming outside of Today's Man all those years ago, that it would lead to the life I have today.

Serendipity translates into the faith that I carry with me daily. The faith that assures me that I am in tune with my gifts, talents, and, ul-timately, purpose in life. According

Faith is taking the first step even when you don't see the whole staircase.
—Martin Luther King, Jr.

to Hebrews 11:1: "Now faith is the substance of things hoped for, the evidence of things not seen."

Faith is the substance that provides evidence to me. Faith is not just a hollow belief or an intellectual understanding that I lean on. It is a willingness that I trust in, rely on, and cling to. The point of holding on to your faith is largely about your ability to trust in things not seen—those things that have not yet matured, those events that have not yet come to pass.

In this fast-paced world, it is easy to get caught up in the desire for positive affirmation from those around us. I have some tough news to share here: you're on a personal journey that is connected to your unique purpose. The truth is that you may not get the affirmation you seek from others. However, I encourage you to always look inward and have faith. Have faith in your gifts (your innate abilities), your talents (those skills you develop), your passion, and purpose.

You may be asking, "What does faith have to do with building proof points?" I'll tell you this: faith will help keep your vision alive and give your passion and dreams substance. Faith and my ability to look inward for support are two essential ways that propel me forward and give me power. They allow me to be open to possibilities instead of constantly questioning myself. Faith also provides me with the confidence and humility to seek out help when I need it.

Pulling in from others

Research has shown that, in the business world, people (especially women) tend to shy away from asking for help. Corporate executives often believe that they have it all together and don't need assistance. Or that asking for help will be viewed as a sign of weakness by the competition. However, similar to looking inward and having faith, I have found that seeking support from others can be a powerful place to be. I believe that pulling in from others is an ongoing part of growth, and it is important to remain humble so that you can be a lifelong learner.

Ranks, titles, or where you sit in the hierarchy simply doesn't matter; you can learn from anyone. Another important factor is that those from whom you seek support will often improve their own skills by helping you. Today, I have more than 10 formal and informal mentoring relationships with people inside of Allstate. I learn as much from my mentees as I try to share with them. Many of these people are younger than I am and are less mature in their careers. However, the benefit is that they are walking a different journey from mine and thus have different experiences to share. As my guidance helps hone their skills, they are at the same time giving me new insights and perspectives as they share their work or stories from their upbringing. Pulling in from others is a mutually beneficial experience that will constantly inform your view, no matter what stage of life you are in.

What words sum up your proof points?

How do you describe yourself or what you do in the world? As we've seen in this chapter, it takes time, energy, and thought to get your message across. Proof points play a key role in illustrating your journey, as they back up what you have to say. They are your evidence.

Let's review what your proof points can be and some of the different ways in which you can establish them.

Redefine what success means to you: your proof points can be those small wins or milestones that you seek to achieve throughout your career. They show that you are on the path to success. Don't focus solely on home runs, as that could lead to frustration. Instead, concentrate on moving forward one step at a time and celebrate those singles that propel you closer to your goals!

Publishing your proof points for your own validation involves writing or telling your stories to others. When I began my Thought of the Day messages, I wanted to share those ideas that inspired me. As the concept evolved, I was able to share my own journey as well as engage with others. The more people who know your story, the bigger your network will become. Your proof points will show others how far you have come, will help you get more recognized, and will leverage more career opportunities.

Proof points are most successful when they are stories that involve those who have helped you along the way. I continually work on my stories to ensure that my message is engaging and compelling. Practice the elements that go into creating a great story and develop a series of your own personal messages that will resonate with different audiences. Work on the stories behind your proof points. Focus on the person who helped you move forward. Write out the highlights of each story. Identify the challenge you faced and how you worked and overcame it to achieve your next level of success.

Remember to look inward. To achieve your milestones, always reach into yourself to pull forth the confidence you need. Know that you have been given a set of talents and gifts that are uniquely yours to share with the world. Use your faith in these gifts to keep on the path, moving forward. You may not always get the affirmation you seek from others, but there is an endless well of encouragement that you can draw from when you recognize the power of faith. Faith in yourself and your abilities will keep your vision alive and provide your dreams with substance.

Always be open and willing to ask for help. It doesn't matter what stage of life you are in. When you are humble and are a lifelong learner, your world will expand exponentially. Seek help at least once a week. There is always someone who can teach you something you don't know. Of course, balance your requests with offers to help others and you have a win-win scenario in your daily work world.

11
Promise 4: Parlay Your Platform

● ●

When I use the term "platform," I am referring to the station in life you've achieved up until this point. I'm including your network of influential people—friends, coworkers, mentors, and even bosses. These are the people who have helped you to accomplish higher goals, just as you've been a part of helping them achieve theirs.

You've created an intangible asset in the form of a personal platform. When I define what makes up a platform, I'm also including your reputation, your relationships, and your experiences. I want to help you magnify this platform and make it as powerful as possible. This chapter will provide a framework to maximize the visibility you have with audiences.

It all begins with character

Your platform is comprised of many things but starts with your character. Character refers to your moral qualities, ethical standards, and principles. The quote from Abraham Lincoln on the next page illustrates that a person's character is what defines him or her. A person's reputation is like a shadow; it changes depending on the position and angle from which you are viewing it. A reputation is a label that others give you; like a shadow, it shifts depending on the opinions of others and, although it comes from your basic nature, it is always unstable and at the mercy of others. Your character is like the tree in that it stays with you for life and is the source for your reputation. Lincoln's quote symbolizes the importance of keeping my values intact and reminds me of how essential it is to maintain my character at all times.

> *Character is like a tree and reputation like a shadow. The shadow is what we think of it; the tree is the real thing.*
> —Abraham Lincoln

Socrates helps us understand how to develop a solid reputation when he said, "The way to gain a good reputation is to endeavor to be what you desire to appear" ("7 Pieces of Wisdom from Socrates," Dumblittleman.com). In other words, act as if you have already achieved your success. Jeff Bezos, the founder and CEO of Amazon.com, also weighs in on how to build your reputation: "A brand for a company is like a reputation for a person. You earn your reputation by trying to do hard things well" (BrainyQuote.com). I will add that the path to building your reputation, and from there your platform, is not an easy path. However, with the help of your network, with their efforts and challenges, you will find you can achieve much faster than going it alone.

When opportunities come up, they tend to go to the people with good reputations. Someone with a good reputation is more likely to get a positive referral and have someone speak confidently on his or her behalf when they are looking for a new job or seeking to advance his or her position within the company. The bottom line is that a good reputation has value and is definitely something you want to have on your side.

Building a good reputation

Many people, as they reach adulthood, do not have much of a reputation or concern themselves with what it may be. Of course, we all know those folks who have done extraordinary things at an early age or who have earned a bad reputation for doing negative things. For the most part, though, there is always time to establish and improve your reputation.

I've discovered that there are some key things you can do to get your reputation moving in the right direction. Let's take a look at some of the ways you can either get your reputation started or improve it.

Imitate those who have earned your respect

Think of the people in your life whom you respect and ask yourself: What is it about them that I respect? What do they do that sets them apart? Why do I see them in such a positive light? Make a list of these people as well as their attributes and then strive to reach them yourself. If you find you're not sure what to do in a situation, ask yourself what you think they would do. If you can, seek out these folks and ask them for advice personally.

Accentuate the positive

I'll admit, this can be harder for some people than for others, but the more you can cut down on any negative talk, the better off you will be. Just like your mother may have said: "If you don't have anything nice to say, don't say anything at all!" A key part of building a good reputation is to focus on the positive in what you say and what you do.

Avoid behaviors that might be considered negative. Though I don't have a specific list of negative behaviors to avoid, my advice is if you're not sure, ask yourself what the people you respect would think of that be-

Thoughts lead on to purposes;
purposes go forth in action;
actions form habits; habits
decide character; and
character fixes our destiny.
—Tyron Edwards

havior. If you do have some habits that may be considered negative, balance them out with more positive ways. Otherwise, you may create a negative reputation that will be hard to overcome.

Take on responsibilities that you can follow through on

When people need things done and you can handle it, volunteer to help and then follow through. *The key here is to follow through.* You can build a bad reputation if you take on something and don't finish it or if you never take on any extra responsibilities. Aim for the middle ground and build a solid reputation by being someone that others can count on. One more point I'd like to make about handling responsibilities: you don't have to brag about your good deeds. In fact, part of having a good reputation is that others will brag on your behalf.

Be involved

An important part of building a good reputation is making sure that people know who you are. Get involved by participating in community and professional events. Increase your connections by introducing yourself to people you don't know and taking advantage of opportunities that allow you to get your name out. If you're not naturally comfortable introducing yourself, then get out there and practice. Volunteer to assist at a youth football camp or get involved in a local charity fundraiser. It doesn't take much effort on your part, but there will be a lot of people in the community who will view you in a positive light because of your involvement in these types of activities. Repeat this process over and over and you'll find that your good reputation builds on itself.

•••••

These are the keys to building a good reputation. If you can work on and improve in the different aspects I've outlined, you will soon start earning a reputation that will have a positive impact in all areas of your life. One more word about building your reputation: constantly protect it. As we've discussed, building a strong reputation is an important component of establishing your platform. Your platform is the sum total of all that you've done to hone your gifts, talents, and skills. It's that sense of confidence and awareness you've grown into and developed by walking the path of life, including insights gleaned from both your personal and professional experiences. You've worked hard for it. Keep it safe.

Inventorying your platform

Believe it or not, "inventorying" is indeed a real word. It usually applies to tangible property and the process of taking an annual inventory of this property. My suggestion is to take an inventory of your intangible assets and check that inventory annually. So what would you consider to be your intangible assets? Here is my list:

- **Your passion (what you want to do).** If you have not done so already, put down your passion in simple words. Write it down or say it aloud to yourself. How does it sound when you say it? Is it clear or ambiguous? Does it make you smile when you say it? Test it out on a few family members and friends. Do they say, "Yep, that's you"? If so, bang! You've probably nailed it. Let's call these your "passion points."

- **Your experiences (what you've done).** We tend to think of only our resume when it comes to explaining our experiences. However, step back for a minute and jot down all of the things you have experienced over the past three months. Consider your primary role at your job, any secondary projects or initiatives you were asked to work on, or work you may have done at your church. Consider any volunteer work you have done with some friends or a trip you have taken. During each of these opportunities, think about what you learned and how they came about. Does this reflect what you had on your resume or does it seem more expansive? It is probably the latter. Now, continue to step back further in time, jotting down the various experiences and what you've learned from each of them. Once you've gone all the way back and created an exhaustive list that covers years, summarize the common experiences into a consolidated list. I'm sure at this point that you're pretty impressed with yourself. Hold on to this feeling; we're going to use it later as we talk about your collage in Chapter 13.

As you compare your experiences to your passion points, are there items you see in your consolidated list that seemingly match your passion? As you identify each of those experiences, highlight them. Now you've created your "passion proofs."

Finally, as you compare your experiences to your passion points, what seems to be missing? Are there things that stand out that you haven't done? Are there any opportunities that you need in order to really be operating within your passion points? Create a small list of those things as well. Let's call those your "passion chasers":

- **Your network (who do you know).** Most of us underestimate the power of our network, but it is truly powerful. For example, take 10 minutes and jot down the names, titles, and experiences of the people you interacted with just yesterday. Include everyone from the time you woke up until the time you went to bed. Quite impressive isn't it? But wait, you're not done yet. Now, go to your LinkedIn account. I'm not going to ask you to write them down, as there are probably too many, but scan through the names, titles, and experiences of those you are linked to. Then go to Twitter, Facebook, and any other social networks you are a part of and do the same. To the extent you have linked, followed, and "friended" people selectively, let's call this your primary network. I'm sure you'll find that it is quite expansive. This is a key component of your platform. An important reminder: don't be afraid to ask for something, and always be willing to give something in return. A thriving network operates like a two-way street.

- **Your reputation (what people say about you).** This is one of the tougher points as most of us don't like to brag about ourselves, but that is not what this is about. Rather, this is about understanding how others view you. Scan through your network again and, as you glance at each name, ask yourself, "What would this person say about me, if asked?"

There is more work you can do here and I would encourage you to do so. Go to some close friends and ask them, "If you could describe me in one word, what would you say?" That will tell you a lot. Write down their answers and be sure to ask several people in many different aspects of your life.

If you already have a job, go back to your performance reviews and scan them. Beyond your performance appraisal, look for words and phrases that also describe you, such as things that define how you work, your personality, and so on. If the performance appraisals don't give you a lot of information, ask for a 360 review. What I mean by this is schedule to speak to your manager, and tell him or her that you are trying to improve your performance and you'd like to get a perspective of how others feel you are doing. These 360 reviews are common at most companies, but if they can't do it, no worries—you have some information to work with.

That's your platform: your passions, your experiences, your network, and your reputation. Now let's pull it all together.

Create a pitch

Let's now think about how to parlay your platform. By parlay, I mean to develop and use what you already have into something else that has a greater value. This greater value is something that you determine and does not necessarily mean something that is worth more (except as it applies to you).

The next step is to ask yourself, "Who would support me in pursuit of my passion? Who in my network would be a valuable asset in getting me from where I are now to where I want to be?" Make a list of those people you could ask for support. You can even consider people who are in your life but who you haven't yet shared your passion with. Write those names down too. Then reach out to anyone you've mentioned.

> *Regardless of age, regardless of position, regardless of the business we happen to be in, all of us need to understand the importance of branding. We are CEOs of our own companies: Me Inc. To be in business today, our most important job is to be head marketer for the brand called You.*
>
> —Tom Peters

Let's take a step back and work to turn this into your pitch. I think of an elevator pitch—named because it should last only as long as a ride in the elevator—as a short, concise way of expressing your passion and who you are. Imagine you get into the elevator on the bottom floor and, just as the doors begin to close, the CEO of the company steps on. It's just the two of you and you've got until the 30th floor to make a good impression. That's your pitch! Developing a good pitch is an essential tool for anyone in business. You need to know how to create one, practice it, and most importantly, how to tweak it for a target audience. It's also vital to know your pitch so well that you can anticipate any questions and respond quickly. Summing up your unique aspects and experiences is one of the most effective ways to engage with others and parlay your platform.

I was helping one of our employees a year ago when she wanted assistance in finding another job. I asked her to give me her elevator pitch. She said she didn't have one so I shared with her these key points to developing a pitch that will "wow" every time.

Develop a pitch

Your pitch is your pronounced way of expressing your passion, your proof points toward it, and what you want to do next to achieve it. Let's try yours. Before you try to write it, however, start here:

My passion is [read from your "passion points"] and so far I've done [read the "passion proofs"] that have helped me pursue it. Now I would like to [read from the "passion chases"] to continue on my journey toward it.

I recommend starting with your passion and provide a quick, wrap-around dialogue to share the reasons why you are who you are and what you do to make a difference.

Keep it fluid

Everyone grows and changes, so your pitch needs to evolve too. If your pitch is outdated and doesn't reflect all that you've done lately, it's time to update it. You know your experiences and passions better than anyone else. Keep track of how you're keeping up with the latest in your business or what sets you apart from the competition. How do you speak about yourself? What highlights do you include and what do you leave out? And more importantly, how do these choices change depending on the audience you're speaking with? The language and approach you use will change over time, and you may choose to highlight a different experience for a particular audience.

Always be prepared

Continually perfecting your elevator pitch ensures that you can always present yourself in the best light. The more you practice, the better you will be at delivery. Try it out on your friends and coworkers. Take their feedback to heart and apply it where necessary. Be prepared so that you're not too comfortable and get caught off guard with a question or concern you hadn't considered.

Ways to parlay your platform

Now that you have an inventory of your platform and are comfortable with your pitch, let's look at the different ways you can build your platform. As I've said before, a platform does many things. In this case, we are going to discuss how you can parlay your platform: how you can use it to give yourself more visibility, allow yourself greater amplification so you can be heard over the noise, and take advantage of any opportunity to make more connections. You can use these different ways to engage and extend your reach even further:

- **Find a mentor.** Find someone who can help you make the best of what you've got to offer, either through a formal program (such as Menttium) or an informal initiative.

- **Seek out volunteer or board opportunities.** One of the most effective ways to parlay your platform is to put your skills and insight to good use within the community. For example, volunteer your services or sit on the board of a non-profit organization.

- **Develop your speaking skills.** Join Toastmasters or a similar program, if you feel you need some practice in learning how to speak to a crowd. If you're already comfortable with your public speaking skills, take advantage of those opportunities to address others. Offer to lead a group discussion or give a PowerPoint presentation.

- **Join internal or external networks.** Many organizations offer internal networks for their employees. Join a group with similar interests or pursue a new avenue to stretch your skills and expertise. You can also find networks within the community as well.

- **Consider more education.** Take additional courses to expand your knowledge or pursue getting certified in your area of expertise.

The home stretch

This chapter sets the stage for the home stretch of the promises. Without addressing how you can parlay your platform, you may end up wasting the efforts you have put into setting up your platform in the first place. Let's review some of the ways you can utilize the platform you have in order to reach even further.

Recognize the importance of your character. You are uniquely yourself. You bring a special set of gifts and talents to every task you do. Your character is that aspect of your personality that will stay with you for life.

Concentrate on building a good reputation. As you move forward in both your professional and personal life, people will form an opinion of you based on your character and reputation. Build a good reputation and protect your standing.

Create an inventory of your intangible assets and review it annually. Your inventory of skills and insights should remain fluid; it grows and develops as you do. Ensure you always know your inventory and can share it at any time. Also, work on a pitch that encapsulates your passion points and experiences.

Lastly, extend your platform by considering further education or certification, developing your public speaking skills, and getting involved in your community.

12

Circle of Influence

● ●

Now that you've established and solidified your platform, this chapter will provide you with some practical insights on what to do next. The key here is to create a balance between and among your circles of influence, control, and concern. When you achieve balance, your platform becomes a powerful stabilizer in this uncertain corporate world where things are always in flux. Let's now focus on how to create an ecosystem where you can thrive—a place where you can mutually give and receive support.

Three circles

Let me start by describing what I mean by these three circles: control, influence, and concern.

My circle of control includes those things that I can absolutely manage directly. These are the areas in my life that I consider hands on. For example, I have control over my reaction to things, my knowledge and experiences, and where and how I invest my time. Professionally, this includes areas such as my budget and the team that I manage.

My circle of influence is largely about people. You know that you can't control others, but you can influence or be influenced by them. In most cases you are going to be very reliant on other people to help you achieve your goals. Therefore, your ability to exert influence on others will be of significant importance.

The next best thing to being wise oneself is to live in a circle of those who are.

—C.S. Lewis

My circle of concern includes those areas that are totally outside of my control and influence. It could be such things as the economy, policies, laws, and so on. Clearly, these are things that I don't have the ability to directly affect or influence materially.

Like it says in the Serenity Prayer, "God grant me the serenity to accept the things I cannot change; courage to change the things I can; and wisdom to know the difference." Imagine that your circles are similarly divided: things you can influence, things you can control, and things you can concern yourself with but have no influence over.

Creating and expanding your circles

Several years ago, around the same time that Ed McGann was questioning me about having my antennas up (as mentioned in Chapter 7), I began creating what I call my grid or ecosystem. Some might call it networking, but to me it is much more than that. It is my ecosystem that in large part reflects those who have an impact on me professionally. Although I have used it as a professional tool, it can certainly be adapted and used outside of work as well.

Developing your ecosystem

The concept is simple. Place yourself in the center box and then work to fill out the eight boxes around you as shown in the following chart:

Mentors/sponsors	Manager/ skip-level manager	Peers of manager and skip-level manager
Management team peers	You	Out-of-department peers
Mentees	Direct Reports and Staff	Peers and contacts outside of the company

- **Directly above you** would be managers. This should include your direct manager and your skip-level manager (your manager's manager). The idea here is to take the relationship beyond the natural focus on the work and tasks involved in your current role. Managers should be enlisted as supporters of your career mobility, actively working with you to assess strengths and opportunities. They should be those people who provide insight and coaching to improve upon the work you currently do as well as act as guidance when you consider different positions in the future.

- **Top left** are sponsors and mentors. Sponsors are a bit different from mentors (although he or she may certainly assist you through the exchange of ideas and coaching). A sponsor is your active advocate. They are typically more senior than you are in the organization and naturally have a broader purview with access to information and people that you don't have. They are the ones to help you in your career mobility, tangibly assisting in finding your next role. A mentor, however, is a person who plays an active role in the exchange of ideas and coaching, both in a professional and, often, personal sense.

- **Top right** are peers of management and skip-level manager. These are the peers of both your manager and your skip-level manager. In other words, they are the people who work closely with your manager and those who work closely with your manager's manager.

- **To your left** are peers on your management team. These are people who report to the same manager that you do.

- **To your right** are peers who are not on your management team, but are from other departments you interact with and whom you have a dependency on in order to execute your projects and initiatives.

- **Bottom left** are mentees, the people to whom you offer guidance and advice.

- **Directly below** you are your direct reports and, broadly, your overall team.

- **Bottom right** are people outside of your organization, whether in your industry or not. It is important to maintain a network of people you can turn to for an outsider's perspective as well as gain insights into things going on in a broader scope. One challenge to always guard against is tunnel vision—that is, being concerned with only what is going on at your company.

Let's put a few names in each of the boxes to help make it real. Perhaps start with two names in each one. Then, color code each box:

- **Red** if you have a "transactional," business-only relationship. This is a less personal relationship and usually focuses on accomplishing specific objectives. For example, the relationship between you and your manager or with a supplier is most often a transactional relationship. These relationships develop around your "go-to" folks, those people you can count on to get things done.

- **Amber** if you have developed an operationally mature relationship. For example, you know they have kids and you know the names of their children. These are people you meet up with every so often and speak with on a semi-regular basis. When you see your relationships developing, you put some effort into getting to know each other better.

- **Green** if you have a fluid relationship. These people are your mentors, colleagues, and close peers. You have coffee or lunch with them regularly and your conversations range from work-related issues to more personal interactions. The discussions that you have with these people are usually related to long-term plans.

Build relationships

So, the question you might be asking is, "Why is this important?" Several years ago, when I was working in HR service delivery at JPMorgan Chase, I thought I was doing great work, and all signs from my immediate manager indicated that I was doing well. At the time, I was highly anticipating getting promoted to senior vice president. As the period for advances approached, I was filled with anticipation. However, to my surprise, the time came and went and I didn't get the promotion.

I reached out to a few folks I knew and asked them to provide me with some constructive feedback. They gave me some great tutelage and offered me advice that I still use to this day. Though it was true I had been doing some great work, the reality was that only one person out of the 10 who made the decisions on promotions was able to speak on my behalf. Advancements were essentially discussed and approved by the HR executive team and, unfortunately, I had not cultivated a relationship with any of them, with the exception of my manager. This was the wake-up call I needed to change that dynamic. I knew I needed to do a better job of sharing my successes and insights with those people who are listed in the top right box. I'll always remember the advice of one of my sponsors: "When your name comes up, you need a majority of people around the table to be familiar with you and your work, giving you the nod."

Coming together is a beginning, staying together is progress, and working together is success.

−Henry Ford

Throughout the next year, I worked on creating better relationships with those I considered within my circle of concern. Not only did I develop new relationships, two of those people moved into my top left box into the role of mentors and sponsors. By continuing to reach out while also keeping up with performing at a high level, I soon reached my goal of being promoted to senior vice president.

Since then, I have continued to use this model and it has served me so well that I have introduced it to others. I'm often asked, "What is the best way to discover and cultivate these types of successful business relationships?" I'm not sure there is a secret weapon here, but the short answer has been to spend time with them. It doesn't matter how determined you are or how hard you work; you can't be a success in business doing it all alone. You know that saying "It takes a village"? Well, it takes a village to help you maximize your potential and achieve your best. The relationships you build are essential to your success. Never forget that fact.

Always look for ways to show the key players in your circle of influence that you value your relationship with them. Give as much as you take and show them you care about what they think and that their opinions matter to you. When you cultivate and expand your circle, it is very rewarding to see your positive relationships develop. The more people there are who care about you, the work you do, and your passion points, the more successful you will be.

Provide influence

Hard work is not always enough. In one recent situation, I was able to influence someone who was supporting my team in a critical support role. This was a person with whom I had a "dotted line" relationship, just as my mentor offered me so many years ago. She was bothered because she was doing the work of peers who were at a level or two higher than she was. I didn't want to lose her talents and got her to talk about the issue from her point of view. I spoke to my peers as well about the situation with this key person. They listened to my concerns, understood my point of view, and shared their concerns. They appreciated my perspective from the point of view of the business, as they were making decisions around promotions on their team. A few months later, the person got promoted—a well-deserved promotion, I might add. Again, it wasn't with my help alone, but through the combination of the person's work and the support she had secured from her direct manager and me as a key client, if you will.

Your personal ecosystem

I often hear people talk about their wish list of folks they'd like to have in their own network. In my opinion, the six degrees of separation seems to be rapidly diminishing. Six degrees of separation is the popular theory that we are all only six people away from every other person in the world. I believe that, given the level of interconnectivity we have access to in this digital age, you are not as far from this wish list of a network as you may think.

It is literally true that you can succeed best and quickest by helping others to succeed.

—Napoleon Hill

In your own personal ecosystem, concentrate on the depth of relationships you develop. These moving parts will help you connect the dots. When you go deep into your ecosystem, you will find a greater interdependence among the many different relationships. And you will find that anything is possible.

In Chapter 15, I offer some suggestions on how to shift those transactional relationships so that you become more deeply engaged with your partners within your ecosystem. For now, let's review what we've covered in this chapter:

- Pay attention to the things you can control, which areas you can influence, and those parts of your life that you have no control over whatsoever. When you achieve a sense of balance, your platform will become more effective and influential. In this unstable corporate environment when things can dramatically change overnight, knowing what you have control over and what you don't is powerful information.

- Create and expand your circles. The best way to begin is to literally create a physical picture of your circle of influence. Work on the diagram shown previously and update that grid consistently. This will provide you with a bird's eye view of your personal ecosystem so you can see where you need to fill in the blanks. Watching those boxes fill up and move around as relationships develop is a rewarding experience as well.

- Nurture your ecosystem to influence your circles of concern. Concentrate on building quality over quantity when it comes to cultivating relationships. Focus on the genuine nature of these relationships rather than just creating contacts with higher level people for material gain. When you do that, you will discover that you're never far removed from developing a key player in your network and that anything is possible.

13

The Collage

● ●

The pit stops we make on the journey—the different encounters we have and the experiences we try on to see if they're a good fit—offer a clear opportunity to pick up a few things along the way. This allows us to form our career/life collage. A collage is an art form that is created by combining small objects (such as bits of paper, cloth, and pictures) onto a surface. Though all of the pieces are separate and seem unrelated, when viewed together they suggest a whole piece. When you see your journey through life similar to the process of creating a fine collage, you can ask, "What elements are missing in order to complete this picture?" This chapter will help you determine that and show you how to leverage your platform to fill in those gaps.

Begin with your canvas

Without a doubt, one of the toughest things I experienced early in my career was realizing that I wanted to be in the C-Suite but having no idea how to get there. I wasn't sure which roles or positions would allow me to make that climb. Naively, I used to wonder, "Hey, if the CEO would just let me hang with him and be his assistant, I could learn everything I'd need to know to take over his job!" We've all seen that in movies, where a CEO or executive adopts a protégé and the protégé gets unbelievable access to the inside view of how the business works. He or she learns all the trade secrets, golfs with the stars, flies around the world, and of course, at some point, takes over the reins of the business. It's a great story, and I'm sure that does happen outside of a Hollywood film stage, but I think those opportunities are few and far between.

Take measured steps

So, what are you supposed to do? You know your passion and can see the destination point, but don't know what steps to take to get there. Let me use the example of a grocery store to illustrate this next point. Imagine walking into a grocery store and finding yourself surrounded by dozens of aisles. Each aisle is filled with numerous categories of food and the choices appear limitless. However, if you just stand there and don't take action, nothing will happen. This is the equivalent of being at work and waiting for something to happen, expecting others to help you drive toward your passion. Now imagine yourself in the same scenario except, this time, you try a different tactic. Instead of standing still, you go down every aisle of the grocery store and randomly grab items off the shelf. There is no method to the madness as you arbitrarily pile your grocery cart high with unrelated items. You probably won't get the desired result, which is the equivalent of taking on any job or role.

Life is a great big canvas, and you should throw all the paint you can on it.

—Danny Kaye

The bottom line is that you need to take measured steps and you have to be deliberate in your choices. This doesn't mean being risk-averse, but it does require looking for things that you believe will be "additive." Something is additive when it adds value to my collection of experiences. Early on in my career, as I looked at various job opportunities, I often viewed jobs as rungs on the ladder to the C-Suite.

If I didn't think it would lead me upward, then I didn't consider it. Through time, however, I have found that perspective limiting and not the right way to look at things.

Add new paint to your collage

I mentioned earlier my experience of working at the recording studio with Taj, a former manager. He was certainly one of those people who made me realize how our experiences in life can be additive and can provide more paint for your collage. Taj had done something that was just outstanding. He had created the financial freedom through real estate and other investments in order to pursue his passion for music. Though he owned the recording studio, renting it out was discretionary, as he wasn't reliant on the income. However, several years after I left the Preverbe recording studio, I made a discovery.

I was headed into a recording studio to work on some songs for a group I had been working with. The building that the studio was located in was one of the more popular music buildings in Philadelphia, as it housed the studio that Joe "the Butcher" Nicolo (a well-known engineer in the hip-hop world) used to manage along with Ruffhouse Records (home of Kris Kross). As I walked past Ruffhouse Records, I saw Taj hanging out in the lobby. I hadn't seen him in more than 10 years! It was great to speak with him again, and we were able to catch up for a few minutes before a guy came out looking for Taj. The man yelled, "Hey, Taj! You missed taking out some of the curse words of the radio edit for the new Kris Kross song." Taj said he would fix it. "Wait a minute," I thought, "What's going on here?"

Taj explained that he had taken a job as a producer/engineer at Ruffhouse Records. As we both had pressing things to take care of (especially Taj, who needed to fix that song!), we didn't get into detail about what I'd just witnessed. I spent the rest of that night puzzling over why Taj would be working for someone else. He had always wanted to do music his way. He wanted to record and publish his own songs, not be working for a record label and two kids who wore their pants backward.

It wasn't until much later that it finally clicked with me what Taj was doing. True to his calling, Taj had created and sustained the financial freedom he needed in order to pursue his passion of music in the way that he wanted; he definitely has his own style. However, Taj recognized the importance of adding value to his collage of music. By working with a record label, he had access to a number of individuals. These were folks who allowed him to further hone his craft of producing and engineering. By being open to this experience, Taj was a better student of the game, and he was closer to the action on a much bigger scale.

Fill in the gaps

We have truly fallen into a "microwave"-oriented society where we want everything immediately. In a digital age that is filled with "overnight" success stories, it is easy to overlook the failure and perseverance it took to achieve those dreams. When we see someone make it big, we tend to only look at that very moment and not fully appreciate that person's journey. One particular example comes to mind.

Anyone who has never made a mistake has never tried anything new.

—Albert Einstein

In the early 1990s, a TV series came on that I really enjoyed called *Roc*. Charles S. Dutton was the star of the show. At the time, it seemed to me that this guy just jumped on the scene, started acting, and away he went. However, I learned that nothing could be further from the truth, as Dutton has one of the most interesting stories you can find.

Born in Baltimore, Maryland, in 1951, Dutton dropped out of middle school to pursue a career as an amateur boxer (his nickname was "Roc"). When he was only 17 years old, Dutton got into a fight, which led to the death of another man. He was convicted of manslaughter and served seven years in prison. After being released, Dutton was arrested for possession of a deadly weapon, so back to prison he went for another three years.

Dutton credits his time in prison with giving him his passion in life. While he was serving this second term, he read a book about black playwrights. This book gave him the idea to start a drama group within the prison, with the purpose of putting on a Christmas talent show for the inmates. He made a deal with the warden: if Dutton agreed to get his GED (General Educational Development), the warden would allow him to start the group. The rest is history, as they say. Dutton got his GED and went on to complete a two-year program at Hagerstown Junior College. Once he was released from prison, he enrolled at Towson State College to pursue a drama degree and then went on to earn a master's degree from the Yale School of Drama. The Tony-nominated and Emmy-winning actor has gone on to perform in many hit plays, television series, and movies. (Source: *http://en.wikipedia.org/ wiki/Charles_S._Dutton.*)

His show *Roc*, which ran from 1991 to 1994, won him an NAACP Image Award. Though most of us may never face some of the challenges he did, it is amazing to watch his passion at work. Dutton took the collage of his life and produced a lifetime of work that stirred me and will no doubt continue to inspire others for generations to come.

Continuously add new color

I discovered that my career was like a canvas, and the experiences I had were colors creating a collage. So, perhaps my experience in accounting put some green on the canvas. My time in human resources put some yellow on the canvas. My time at the hardware store put some blue on, and my time in HR service delivery added some orange. Although those were great experiences, that's only four colors. For the direction I wanted to head in, my collage needed to be much more diverse and colorful.

Once I got comfortable with that, I was faced with the reality that I didn't know what I didn't know. In other words, I didn't know what colors I might need for my collage to advance my journey. I was reminded of the great story in the movie *The Karate Kid*.

The point that really struck home with me about this movie came through the character of Daniel, as he seeks to understand how to become great at his passion: karate. He goes to Mr. Miyagi for help as this is someone trustworthy and experienced at what Daniel wants to do. Mr. Miyagi agrees to help, but Daniel has to trust him to get the help he needs. More importantly, Daniel has to maintain his trust through a series of training exercises that do not appear to be linked to his goal. However, once he puts it all together, he realizes that the time he has spent honing these foundational skills have led him to become great at karate.

Don't let what you can't do stop you from doing what you can do.
—John Wooden

I find the same to be true for me as I pursue my passion. I've been blessed to get input from others who have had great achievements and careers, and, when seeking my next learning opportunity, I have benefited from their counsel. These people often share with me a different way to view an opportunity that I may not have initially seen. Today, I am in a different place from where I began. I no longer just look for the next rung on the ladder to climb, but rather seek out the next learning opportunity to add more color to my collage.

Find other painters

I've shared with you my experience of choosing to make a lateral career move at the bank. I was willing to lose the corner office and appear to be at a lower-level job so that I could fill in those missing areas on my own career collage. At that time, I needed to generate experience on the revenue-producing side of the business, and this was the best way to achieve that goal. Such moves can be very humbling; this certainly was the case for me. I knew that, in order to move up and out, I needed to take a position that appeared lower. Sometimes, you just have to be a student of the game and be open to returning to what some would call a "Beginner's Mind."

I love to unlock the secrets of others' expertise. I often call on colleagues, peers, and mentors when they are exceptionally well versed in a particular area that I am less knowledgeable about. I'll open with, "Hey, here's a student-of-the game question: how do you go about your [topic/area of expertise]?" This kind of question gives them the license to talk long and deep about their area of expertise. The ability to ask this type of question comes from being comfortable with where you are in life. It can feel vulnerable to admit that you don't know something. At the same time, that's the best way to learn! The more you grow, the more you realize what you don't know. You learn to appreciate others who are well versed on their topics and welcome them into your circle.

Enjoy the process

One of the key components of platform leverage is the development of our skill sets, competencies, and experiences. Up close, many of your experiences may not make sense. When you step back, however, you can pick out how certain areas came together to create the collage that makes up your life. Here are some of the ways you can prepare your life as a long-term collage and how to enjoy the process as it unfolds.

Be open to possibilities, like a brand-new canvas. When I first started, I knew what I wanted to achieve but didn't know what path to take to get there. You may be in a similar situation right now. The best thing you can do is be flexible enough to know that you have a lot to learn; be receptive to taking in your experiences and making the most of them.

As you step out onto your path, don't be afraid to take a risk or get caught up in "paralysis by analysis." Be thoughtful about the choices you make to ensure that you continue moving forward.

Just remember, sometimes a lateral move is necessary and, though it may look like a setback, as long as you have your long-range goal in mind, embrace the opportunity to add color to your collage.

Consider what colors you need on your collage as you journey toward your passion. When I realized that my collage needed to be more diverse, I had to accept the reality that there was plenty I didn't know. In order to add more rich hues to my collage, I had to be willing to seek out other painters to help me expand.

Learn with patience and optimism. Adding depth and color to your collage will require you to remain a lifelong learner. Always be ready to be a student. Keep a positive attitude and continually ask yourself, "What am I learning from this situation? What is my takeaway from this lesson?" All of your experiences collectively will add texture and dimension to your collage.

14

Promise 5: Put It Into Action

• •

New Year's resolutions such as losing weight or getting more organized often wither and die by the middle of February. This is because it takes time and continued effort for newer commitments to form into habits. This chapter will add to and recap the collection of practical tools, tactics, and techniques you've gathered throughout the previous chapters. We'll also discuss how essential it is to take risks in life in order to drive toward professional and personal success. All of these efforts combined will move you from the planning stage into action, from new commitment to old habit.

The only way this will work is if you commit to taking some actions on a regular basis. You can do this by planning, acting, reviewing, adjusting, re-planning, and repeating these steps in a continuous cycle. I can provide a framework for this, but if you don't commit to doing it then it won't matter.

A plan in action

James 2:14–16 is one of my favorite pieces of scripture and reads as follows:

What good is it, my brothers and sisters, if someone claims to have faith but has no deeds? Can such faith save them? Suppose a brother or a sister is without clothes and daily food. If one of you says to them, "Go in peace; keep warm and well fed," but does nothing about their physical needs, what good is it?

So the question becomes, If you believe it, are you ready to commit to it? If you have a plan but aren't willing to see it through, what does it matter? One of my favorite examples of commitment and perseverance is the story of Rick and Dick Hoyt. I've seen their story on YouTube more times than I can remember, and I am always touched by their commitment and love every time I see it.

I have been impressed with the urgency of doing. Knowing is not enough; we must apply. Being willing is not enough; we must do.
—*Leonardo da Vinci*

The story starts with Dick Hoyt's infant son Rick developing cerebral palsy as a result of his umbilical cord getting wrapped around his neck at birth. Today, precautions could most likely have prevented this tragic outcome. But this was in 1962 and, unfortunately, this was an outcome both Dick Hoyt and his wife had to adjust to—a lifetime of caring for a dependent son. When doctors recommended that Rick should be institutionalized, they both adamantly refused. Instead, they took their son home to raise him as normally as they could.

Many parents would have never thought of getting their physically challenged son into a regular sporting activity. But this family was no ordinary one. What started as running one race turned into two and, from there, Rick Hoyt and his father kept going. Now, 1,000 marathons and triathlons, and 27 years later, this is a permanent and wonderful part of the Hoyt family's life. Rick, who is unable to talk or walk, graduated from high school and went on to Boston College. There he worked to earn a degree in special education. Rick taught for a year and then transitioned into a job in computers. In fact, Rick was part of a team that developed the "Eagle Eyes" computer system for Boston College that helps

Dick communicate. (Source: *http://sports.espn.go.com/oly/news/ story?id=2631338.*)

Consider all of the work the Hoyt family has put into this: the training, the modifications to their equipment, and so on. I hope this story has inspired you as you consider putting your plan into action. Let's keep going and work together to get this done. I promise you it will be very rewarding and not nearly as physically taxing as what the Hoyts had to go through!

A real decision is measured by the fact that you've taken a new action. If there's no action, you haven't truly decided.
–Tony Robbins

Putting your system in place

In their book, *Execution*, authors Larry Bossidy, Ram Charan, and Charles Burck discuss a number of leaders whom they speak of positively as it relates to great execution. They summarize the three core processes of execution as strategy, people, and operations. Let's consider what you've done so far. Strategy refers to identifying your passion and some of the things you can do to achieve that passion. People are those folks in your network and who you see daily. This next section will be about operations and how to ensure you get things done.

Create your passion point incubator

Here are some things you can do to produce your passion point incubator:

- **Outline your passions** and where they intersect with your gifts and talents. Initially, just write down those dreams you want to chase; don't worry about being concise, accurate, or profound. Close your eyes and go back to your childhood if necessary, but get in touch with your passion. Try to narrow the list down to two or three passions. I certainly don't want to constrain you, but I want to caution that more than three might splinter your focus.

- **Add depth to your passions.** Next to each passion, write down a few points on how you feel about it. What is it that gets you stoked about each passion? What would success look like for each one?

- **Create a list passion partners.** By each of your passions, write down a few names of people who are currently doing what you admire. It could be people you know personally or not. Set a goal of three people for each passion, with at least two you have access to.

- **Engage your passion partners and create direction**. Using the list of names you've just developed, challenge yourself to meet with each one individually over the next 30 days during breakfast, lunch, or dinner if possible. During this meeting, you want to accomplish four things:

    1. Share the journey you've recently been going through with this book, and how you've crystallized your passions and made a commitment to

pursue them. Explain that you see them as operating within their passions and you would value their input.

2. Ask them to share their story and how they got into their passion.

3. Share what you have done to date and ask them for two to three pieces of advice to help you follow a course toward your passion.

4. Ask their permission to follow up with them regularly in order to provide updates and continue getting their advice.

- **Create the flexibility to pursue your passions.** Review the different aspects in your life: finances, personal commitments, professional commitments, how you use your free time, and so on. Identify those things that could deter you from truly chasing your passion.

Create a living learning and development plan

Using the learning and development diagram plan on page 185 as a guideline, let's complete it together as follows:

- **Ownership.** Write your name at the top left of the form. Directly under it, enter today's date as the Start Date. Over to the right edge of the paper write down your Passion Point Date. Choose the date based on what you feel is realistic; it could be one year, three years, five years, or more. If you have no idea, let's go with one year, as this puts pressure on you to drive forward and can always be adjusted later. For years, as I've watched football games (I'm a huge Washington Redskins fan and whatever team my son is playing for), my wife has always been aggravated over how much urgency the losing team seems to put into the last five minutes of a game. I didn't get it at first and, as a former athlete, would always try to rationalize the behavior. But then I stepped back and noticed the same thing happens in basketball games and other sporting events. I noticed, too, that the same thing happens at work as the year comes to a close. A part of our human behavior is to react and place urgency on upcoming deadlines and due dates; it's just the way we are wired. So keep that in mind when you are selecting a date. Just don't push the date too far out.

- **Passion Point column.** Under this column, enter each passion point on a separate row.

- **Work and Experiences column.** Jot down the work you've done to date and are doing now using macro statements. It could be job titles, function titles, or a short description of the work. Write each one down in the row it closely aligns to in terms of your passions. If it doesn't align with one of your passions, write it down near the bottom of the column. It's also okay to list items in more than one row if something you do meets more than one passion.

- **Free Time column.** Similar to the last column, write down what you typically do with your free time. When you're not working or spending time with your significant other, what are you doing? Use the same approach here as well: write each one down in the row it closely aligns to in terms of your passions.

- **Learning Opportunities column.** Based on your passion writing exercise, as you looked at the intersection of the passion, your gifts, and your talents, did you find everything matching up perfectly? Probably not. But if they do, you are likely already operating within your passion and I'll invite you to help me write the next book—drop me a line! Also, what did your passion partners tell you? Write down these learning opportunities.

Name:		Passion Date:	
Passion Point	Work and Experiences	Free Time	Learning Opportunities

Now, step back and look at what you have in front of you. Hopefully you'll see a much clearer and comprehensive picture than before you started. What you've developed should show you how to better align your time with your passions and what opportunities (such as learning experiences, taking classes) might guide you toward your passion point. From here, how you pursue those opportunities can take many different forms.

As mentioned in the previous chapter, complete the ecosystem chart and write down at least two names in each of the eight boxes. Note that you shouldn't only put those who you feel will be easiest to get along with. In order to have a triangulated feedback system, you need some people who have a different point of view, demeanor, and outlook than yours. Diversity matters.

Create an engagement plan

This is one of the most critical parts. It won't just happen; you need to plan in advance how often you will engage with these folks. For example, next to each person's name, it can be as simple as writing down bi-weekly, monthly, bi-monthly, or quarterly. Your meetings might go something like this:

- **First meeting.** It might feel awkward at first, but plan in your initial meeting to find some common ground and let the conversation flow from there.

- **Second meeting.** If it feels appropriate, share your passion with the person and what you are doing to drive toward it. Connect the dots for him or her relative to your current work and let the conversation continue naturally from there. You'll often find that people will have some sort of reaction. They will either be intrigued, making them think about their own passions, or they'll have advice to share. The goal here is to drive up the engagement between you.

- **Third meeting.** You hopefully have a level of comfort with each other at this point. Now is the time to continue the discussion, but also to let him or her know that you'd like help. That help can range from input on your performance, to guidance on your journey toward your passion point. You'll have to feel that out based on what you learn about the person, as well as his or her receptiveness during your conversations.

One of the things we often say is that we don't have time to engage with people. Find the time. For example, when you look at the ecosystem chart you completed, there should be at least 18 names there. Most of us think, "I don't have the time to meet with 18 people on a regular basis." I'm going to push back and say that you actually do. I am going to remind you of what I mentioned in the previous chapter: don't eat breakfast and lunch alone. Invite these folks to join you. Assuming that you're gone for two weeks each quarter—between time out of the office and travel—that leaves 10 weeks or 100 opportunities for breakfast and lunch. There you go!

Plan the calendar. Schedule the meetings in advance, or place them on a spreadsheet and schedule the get-togethers as they get closer. Schedule three things: 1) your "catch-up meetings" with your ecosystem/circle of influence; 2) your quick review time; and 3) your quarterly planning time.

Deal with the risks

Nelson Mandela once said, "A good head and a good heart are always a formidable combination." Who better than Mandela to quote as we consider risk? His life offers so many powerful lessons. Mandela's commitment to justice, and the risks he took to envision and create a better future for his country, for its current and future generations, have been an inspiration for generations around the globe.

Putting this action plan in place will not only require assertive-
.ness, planning, and resilience, but also going outside of your comfort zone. You'll need to buck tradition, do the non-conventional,
and even defy logic as you learn to trust your gut.

Previously, I shared my story about looking for a new role in
JPMorgan Chase some years ago. I outlined the process I initiated
and how I went around the company meeting with the heads of
the various lines of business. What I didn't mention is that I was
initially reluctant to do so and even a bit scared. It was nerve-
wracking to imagine all of the different possibilities. I asked myself, "Will they reject seeing me? What will they think of me? Am
I overstepping my bounds in asking to meet with them?" You get
the picture.

I eventually worked up the courage to pursue these conversations. It actually proved to be a very enlightening experience for
many reasons. I learned new aspects of the business (which was
my original goal), but I also learned a lot about the executives I
met with. I learned about their habits, receptivity, and adaptability. One executive in particular told me that he would love to meet
more people within the company, but that the company was just
too large, making this impractical. He went on to say, however,
that when people did reach out to him, it displayed courage and he
felt compelled to meet with them.

So what is risk, anyway? There is going to be a different definition for each of us. Let's try to put it in perspective as we think
about how to overcome it. As Mandela said, if we have a head and
heart committed to pursuing our passions and giving back, what
can deter us? Also, let's be honest, the challenges and risks we are
talking about are typically not equal to the risks of physical im-
prisonment that Mandela experienced.

Here are a couple of specific areas of risk that could come into
play as you put things into action:

- **One might be the perception risk.** Similar to my previous story, you may risk that some people will see you as overly ambitious if you wander outside the norm. In the story I shared earlier in Chapter 3 of my conversation with Tony, there was certainly risk that I would be perceived as not being a team player, but rather highly focused on my own career.

- **Another risk might be financial,** the feeling that you might be putting your current job or possibilities in jeopardy as you favor and work to choose things aligned with your passions. That may translate to a potential reduction or loss of income. This is certainly true. Again, as in the story I shared in Chapter 3, that situation could have taken a turn for the worse with me possibly losing my job. However, there are two things I want to point out, both in the here and now and for the long term. As it relates to today, the reality is that employers don't owe you a job. That said, even if you do everything you are asked, it does not guarantee you a permanent job. You can arrive to work any day and find that your job is gone and that you are simply terminated. It could be part of a full-blown reduction in force or just that your services are no longer required. In terms of employment, most U.S. states follow what is called "employment at will," which simply means an employee can be dismissed for any reason, without having to establish "just cause," and without warning. The second thing I would point out is for the long-term game. In the first chapter, I mention that most of us will spend more than 7 million minutes of our lives related to work. If that is going to be the case, don't you want most of those 7 million minutes spent on something you are passionate about? I know what my answer to that question is; do you?

Manage your risks

For years, risk for me was driven by fears of inadequacy, with roots that extended back to my childhood. Not unlike most young boys, I looked for approval and validation from of my father. Having never received that, I tended to always question myself. I often got caught up in thinking less of myself and assumed that others did as well. I've had to learn how to cope with it. I use the word "cope" purposely because even today, as I write this book some 20-plus years later, I'm not sure I can say, "I'm over it." However, I'm more aware of my feelings and when certain emotions rise, I can spot them, see them for what they are, and coach myself through rough waters. That in and of itself is a major accomplishment and helps me manage my "risk of not being accepted."

Courage is the mastery of fear, not the absence of it.

—Mark Twain

At any given moment, most of us have a goal or two we'd like to aim for that requires some degree of risk. It may be a job change or starting a whole new career. The act doesn't have to major; even asking for a raise can be uncertain! However, I will warn you that the easiest move is to do nothing. And though it might feel better than those dangerous feelings that risk evokes, the good feelings are only temporary. You will still need to accept risk in order to move forward. I encourage you to write down the risk and the perceived consequences of what could happen from taking it. This list should include the highest upshot and the lowest downside, with everything else in between.

Now go back and choose the most likely consequences, and let each scenario play out in your mind. Ask and answer these questions: "What if this happens? How will I handle this?" Your answers will help to clarify how you would deal with the consequences. Include how you can leverage your platform to minimize the risks and provide a softer landing if things don't turn out well.

Track your progress

Track your progress; adjust and prioritize on a quarterly basis. It's very important to document the progress along your journey. Just as Rick Warren's quote says, it's vital that you see how far you've come. There are a few things to document:

- **Proof points and gaps.** Are you seeing progress toward your passion? If so, what are the proof points? If not, what do you need to change? Are you closing the gaps identified between today and your passion point? If so, how? If not, what do you need to change?

- **Risk-taking.** Were there any perceived risks or barriers you encountered during the quarter? How did you approach them?

- **Engagement.** Did you have a meaningful engagement with some of the folks in your ecosystem? If so, how would you describe it? Make a few notes about each person in your ecosystem/circle of influence.

- **Feedback/coaching.** What feedback and coaching have you received from others? Did you nurture your network? Is your network triangulated and balanced? Did you expand your network?

Discuss your findings with your incubator team and get their feedback. Then, plan out the next quarter. Start with what you need to do that you haven't been doing. Stop with the things that you expected would help in your journey, but don't appear to be producing the results you want. Additionally, regarding time management, deterrents, and distractions, ask yourself, "What discretionary things continue to take up my time and make no contribution to my journey?" Stop them. Lastly, continue with things that are working well!

Let's review some of the practices that will help build the "muscle memory" required to form the habits you need to successfully move forward on your journey.

Knowledge is great, if acted upon. You don't just need to come up with a plan; you need to be committed and see it through. Take advantage of the outlines listed previously to get you started on a concrete plan. Mobilize a team to help you through your journey. You'll need their input and encouragement as you strive toward your goals.

Remember how far you've come, not just how far you have to go. You are not where you want to be, but neither are you where you used to be.

—Rick Warren

Understand your perceived risks and work toward managing them. It's useful to work through what your risks are and how you are going to deal with them. Ask yourself, "What is the worst thing that can happen if I take this action? What is the worst thing that can happen if I don't take this action?"

Track and assess your progress regularly. Be flexible and open to adjusting the next set of actions required for improving your results. Include your network in this process and use any feedback or constructive criticism to motivate you.

15

Promise 6: Practice Philanthropy

• •

Give. You can never go wrong with giving, even when nobody hears about it. Giving not only helps the one you reach out to, it helps you as the giver find purpose and encourages you to make giving a lifelong habit. So many of us have benefited from the gifts of others, and you never know what a small, or even not-so-small, gift might mean to someone in need. As you begin to find success in life, make giving a habit commensurate with your earnings.

Philanthropy is defined as "goodwill to fellow members of the human race; especially an active effort to promote human welfare." Philanthropy can come in so many forms. Often, you may associate it with organizations such as the Bill and Melinda Gates Foundation or with Warren Buffet, giving billions away in support of education, world health, and other community endeavors. We tend to think about museums, missions trips, and many larger-than-life efforts to improve our society. And that's all right, but I tie it back to four things: family, friends, community, and society.

Giving starts at home

As I mentioned in Chapter 1, for years I watched my mother and father act as foster parents for many children when I was younger. I'm not totally sure what the drive was, as my parents were certainly busy enough already with my father being an insurance agent and pastor of a small church and my mother working as a legal secretary. However, for a long period of time, we always seemed to have a foster child in the home, and none of them were without their challenges.

From what we get, we can make a living; what we give, however, makes a life.
—Arthur Ashe

I had a foster brother for a while named Mark. I am not sure what Mark's background was, but he often ended up in some kind of trouble. My parents had strict curfew rules. For example, I had to be in by dark. Often, as the sun went down, I could hear my mom calling from the door, "Bernie..." and I knew it was time to head in.

The older guys had later curfews. But no matter what it was, Mark would break it on occasion. My parents put the extra locks on the door once the last curfew time for the evening was hit, which meant you had to ring the bell to get in. Mark would often come home with an interesting story. One night he arrived with a bag of groceries in his hand as he knocked on the door, asking for forgiveness. I have no idea where the bag full of groceries came from or where he got the money to pay for them.

I had a foster sister named Stacy who lived with us for a short time. We never built a strong relationship, as she seemed to just bounce in and out of the house. One day we came home from an outing (Stacy had not gone with us) and found our house had been robbed. From speaking with neighbors, it sounded like Stacy had engineered the entire thing, letting some people she knew into the house through the basement window.

There were several other foster brothers and sisters I had, some of whom I knew better than others. As I mentioned, Ivan Bonner was the one I knew best, as he stayed the longest. Despite all of these experiences with different children in and out of our lives, I saw my mother and father love these kids in an incredible way. Though they did not look past shortcomings or abide by rules being broken, they did not let it deter them. Both of my parents would press on and work toward helping those children. That is a powerful demonstration of giving back!

Give and receive

My passions are music, helping others, and innovation. As you've seen through the various stories I've shared from my journey, I have benefited tremendously from the wisdom provided by many people. This is just a snapshot of how it stacks up for me:

- I could say countless things about my mother, but most relevant to this book is that she showed me what the work ethic is about: holding down two or three jobs at a time while trying to keep our lives unshaken after her and my father divorced. She also showed me the value of investing in myself.

- Ms. Lee, my sixth grade teacher, taught me not to settle for less than my best for myself.

- Joe Jankowski gave me my first experience working in a retail environment and service business. He taught me how to make keys, fix windows and screens, do light plumbing and light electrical, and other things. He also taught me how to work the cash register and take inventory. When I was 16, he trusted me to run the store, close it for him during the week after school, and often open for him on Saturdays.

- Robert "Taj" Walton showed me how to live for passion in music.

- Don Fleming gave me my first opportunity to work in a corporate office environment, helping me transition from being a security guard in a Today's Man store, to working in the Today's Man corporate offices. He gave me exposure, while I was working in accounting, and he allowed me to help his team with new store openings. He gave me the chance to teach the new store team how to set up the security system and the cashier management team how to process payroll.

- Barry Pine showed me what it looked like to stand by your principles, morals, and ethics, and that doing so was more important than being popular.

- Susan Highfield was my first manager at WSFS Bank. She hired me and allowed me to use my payroll skills, but also gave me a broader role with responsibility for the HRIS system (although I hadn't done that before). This allowed me to reach back into my computer learning center training and my passion for innovation, and develop the system to move WSFS into the future from an HR systems perspective.

- Vicky Myoda (Susan Highfield's successor) shepherded my learning in human resources in a much broader sense. She coached me through learning compensation and HR generalist duties. She also coached me through doing new hire check-ins, exit interviews, worker's compensation claims, and much more.

- Skip Schoenhals mentored me through the creation of my business plan for my record label. I wanted to do a Christian hip-hop label and was working on the business case with a group in Philadelphia, but Skip took interest, read it, and introduced me to some venture capitalists so I could pitch it. His view as a CEO of a bank was invaluable. This was such a great opportunity for me in my early 20s.

- Steve Hallett coached me through my first opportunity to manage a large team upon joining NovaCare. Prior to this experience, I had only managed a team of two—me and an assistant at WSFS. In this new role, I had a team of 20 or more, with three supervisors reporting to me. In addition, Steve allowed me to trust my gut. He would listen to my plans and provide his input, but would never make me do it his way. He let me make mistakes and learn from them. He also coached me through a number of scenarios as NovaCare split off and created NovaCare Employee Services, a separate entity. This was a great learning opportunity to use my experience in payroll and HR operations, but shift it from an expense focus to a revenue-generation focus.

- Brenda Snipes helped convince me to take a consulting role at Transaction Information Systems. Up until then, I worked in what I considered to be stable corporate roles and consulting felt very risky to me. Brenda coached me on how to assimilate the distinct differences between ramping up in a corporate role versus a consulting assignment. She also showed me the importance of demonstrating value early in a consulting gig.

- Lisa Neal-Graves taught me not to take the "platinum handcuffs." She was great at pushing me to think outside the box and do the unexpected, starting with the first interview. When Lisa called me about the opportunity to be the payroll operations manager at Chase, I initially wasn't going to even entertain it, as I had just accepted a job offer at ADP. However, Lisa continued to push and pique my curiosity, so much so that I drove up to New York to meet with her the next day. During my time with her, she challenged us to be "P.I.G.S."–People Involved in Greatness. She didn't have a background in what I did, but she understood operations at a macro level, provided me with her view of how to operate in a Chase context, and gave me the space to do it my way.

She was a great communicator and had that knack for taking large, complex problems and communicating them in simple ways, along with creating a lexicon for those who remained with us—a trait that I value to this day as I strive to do the same.

- Enza Carone helped me pace myself. I was (and still am) very ambitious, and Enza was great at helping me focus on the most important things and avoid the feeling that I had to do it all. As I watched how she operated, I noticed that prioritization was a key element in her own success. She was purposeful in her time management and geared the processes around her in that way. Even when she responded to e-mail, she had a system where her administrative assistant knew which e-mails would be important versus those that could wait to be printed out for Enza to skim through on her train ride home. This was before we all had blackberries and iPhones!

- Jennifer Cavazzini pushed me to get out of my comfort zone, both in the work I was managing and in my communication and leadership style.

- Anya Tomko taught me strategic multi-tasking. She had one of the broadest set of responsibilities I had seen, yet had the capability to understand each of them.

- Claude Weir (head of employee relations and HR executive for the investment bank at JPMorgan Chase) taught me how to navigate the organization.

- Kim Davis (Aunt Kim, as I often call her) taught me the importance of being authentic.

This list could go on and on as what I've shared here is just the tip of the iceberg, both in the number of names listed as well as the depth of the relationships and what I've learned from them.

Align your giving with your passion

As the saying goes, "To whom much is given, much is required." I'm not sure when that clicked for me, but through time I've learned that giving back to others is core to my very being. It is a part of who I am. Absent doing it, there is a void.

For me, the opportunity to operate with a philanthropic mind-set is virtually limitless. When you give from your passion, you will find pure pleasure. It won't be "work." When considering volunteering activities (such as community work or serving on a board), follow your passions. That way, it will feel less like an obligation and more like a privilege.

Holy Culture and Corelink Radio

As you'll recall, Corelink Radio and my joining Holy Culture were born out of my passion to see youth exposed to an alternative to the hip-hop music they often hear on the radio. It's so interesting now as they both have similarly defined mission statements. Here are their current mission statements:

- Holy Culture, L.L.C. operates *www.holyculture.net* and *forum.holyculture.net*, providing media for the general consumer, tools and resources for artists, and serves as an advocate for the Christian hip-hop genre. Holy Culture's mission is to "connect, collab and inspire. We exist to promote Christ, serve the Christian community and provide tools to those that co-labor in the culture. We cover hip-hop, rock, CCM (Contemporary Christian music), alternative, rhythm & praise and gospel."

- Corelink Radio operates under Corelink Ministries, a 501c ministry. Its mission tagline is "Linking the world to the Word." Corelink exists to provide youth with a positive alternative that is counter to the current, pervasive culture through *www.corelinkradio.com* and mobile apps, providing 24×7 streaming of Christian hip-hop and rhythm and praise music. Further, Corelink believes in revitalizing communities through Christian hip-hop music, with the long-term objective of driving programming penetration through AM/FM, Satellite radio, and streaming media (such as Pandora). To accomplish this long-term objective, Corelink needs to provide proof that such a market exists. It does this through creating a strong listenership base and a cost-benefit analysis that it can share in secular markets.

Both of these passions are far from where they were when the journey started. As I began operating in Christian hip-hop, I was a rapper, DJ, and producer, initially consumed (like most) with trying to express myself through music and creating a listener base. I soon figured out that there was a whole community of folks trying to do that same thing, and many of them were talented in their own right. However, what appeared to be lacking was a platform to share that music with the broader community, be it the Christian and Church community, or secular youth. It weighed on me for quite a while as I thought, "Which would really be more beneficial? Should I continue rapping and producing my own music, or should I work to create a platform to support this community?" I chose the latter.

> We are all gifts to each other, and my own growth as a leader has shown me again and again that the most rewarding experiences come from my relationships.
>
> —Michael Dell

Things just began to roll from there. My brother-in-law and I started Corelink Radio, renting airtime on an AM station in Camden, New Jersey. It allowed us to hone our skills, interview local groups, and establish a reputation in the area. From there we moved to podcasting on Holy Culture (I wasn't an owner at the time), allowing our show to be heard around the world.

Through the years, I was offered the opportunity to join Holy Culture as a co-owner. I jumped at the chance because it matched my passion to help this community, as, at that time, Holy Culture owned and operated *forum.holyculture.net* and *www.holyculturedownload.com* (HCD), the largest online Christian hip-hop store.

I thought the forum was unique, bringing together a community of people who were interested in impacting the hip-hop culture through music—a place for dialogue on a number of fronts.

Everything from the serious (theological debates) to the insig-nificant (sports) has been and continues to be discussed on the forum. More importantly, it has allowed for the creation of many long-standing relationships within the community.

The HCD store was even more unique, as this was before iTunes was born. At the time, it was difficult to find Christian hip-hop music and thus HCD became a source for many people to turn to for music. A few years into it, my partner had the idea of creating *www.holyculture.net* as a broader media Website, offering news, album reviews, interviews, free music, and videos to the commu-nity. It was the natural evolution of our brand.

We both thought (and sometimes continue to think) that this could be a nice, profitable business. However, to date, it has been anything but that. Although this has been frustrating at times, I have gained so much in terms of my passion for music and in help-ing others. Over the past several years we have had the honor to serve:

- Hundreds of artists: from the most popular touring art-ists such as Lecrae, to the brand-new one who wants an opportunity to share his or her first song. We have had the chance to counsel countless artists through various aspects of their career: from how to initiate and grow their ministries, to business matters such as selling their music online or gaining distribution.

- Parents: We've had parents come to us, asking for sug-gestions on how to introduce their children to positive music and experiences.

- Youth: Through the hosting and offering of free music downloads on our Website, we've been able to help curi-ous youth quickly build a collection of music that feeds their newfound interest or continues to edify and build on their more mature interest.

- Church leaders: We have helped a number of church leaders connect with artists to perform at venues and provide music for their youth programs.

All of this is far more than I had ever expected. These platforms have allowed me to play an instrumental role in countless lives.

To know even one life has breathed easier because you have lived. This is to have succeeded.
—*Ralph Waldo Emerson*

As we continued to develop our online presence, we also recognized the need to provide "physical music" to people, whether directly from us or from others who want to affect our youth and the hip-hop culture evangelistically. A few years ago, we developed the Drop CD (*www.holyculture.net/drop*), a tool that we provide to people who would like to connect with others in person. We found that such a tool provides a platform for conversation. As people "drop" the free CD on people, they often ask them to listen to a track or two while they are together, or offer an explanation of what they are about to hear. Getting that dialogue started is the key to a potentially great relationship.

Nothing is as important as the act of giving—giving your time, energy, and support to others. While you're making plans to pursue your passion, you can also make big plans to have a real impact on the lives of many by practicing philanthropy. Anybody can do small deeds on a daily basis, and I encourage you to make whatever changes you can and develop a lifelong habit of giving.

Teach others how to give by modeling that behavior. No matter what stage of life you are in, you can model practicing philanthropy. I learned from many of my colleagues and mentors firsthand the power of changing the world through giving.

Start by aligning your giving with your point of passion. When you do this, you will find pure pleasure and it won't feel like work. I have committed countless time and resources to pursue my passion with Holy Culture and Corelink Radio, and yet the reward of touching the lives of people I've never met all across the world is greater than I could have ever imagined. That is the power of giving!

Index

About the Author

● ●

James currently serves as executive vice president and president of LegalShield B2B Solutions with oversight for the brokerage, affinity, and small business divisions in addition to developing new, innovative channels, and products.

Prior to joining LegalShield, James served as the president of Allstate Affinity Solutions where he launched innovative partnerships with Bass Pro Shops, United Airlines, Intercontinental Hotels Group, Office Depot, and the Fuel Rewards Network, differentiating Allstate in the insurance industry, driving customer acquisitions, loyalty, and revenue growth.

Prior to Allstate, James served as a senior vice president at JPMorgan Chase Card Services where he was responsible for Affinity and Co-brand partner relationships. His responsibilities included profitable growth, marketing, partnership rationalization, and the oversight of a number of partnerships that included

AARP, AAA, La Quinta Hotels, New York Life, Notre Dame, Subaru, and the military branches of service. During this time, he was able to drive significant profit increases through increased consumer acquisitions and retention, product improvements, increased wallet share, and improved underwriting.

Before that, James served as the HR service delivery North America Executive, responsible for providing seamless services to employees, managers, and HR business partners. In this capacity, he played a leadership role in mergers, acquisitions, and divestitures; the establishment of a captive off-shoring hub in India; and numerous operational and technology transformations.

With more than 20 years of professional experience, his areas of leadership experience include revenue generation, B2B relationship development, finance, technology, operations, human resources, and services, with experience in financial services, healthcare, and retail.

James holds a BS in business management from the University of Phoenix. He is actively involved in community and youth based activities. *Success on Your Own Terms* is his first book.

James has a wife of 17 years, Aishah, and a son, James B. Rosseau, Jr.

Support for the journey...

Speaking engagements

As you now know, helping others is my chief passion. If you believe that I can be of service to you and your group (e.g. youth group, book club, church, employee network group, leadership team, etc.), I would be honored to visit with you. Simply, I am more than happy to come speak at your school group, church group, office, etc. Please visit *www.jamesrosseausr.com* and use the contact form.

Tools

Whether this is about your personal journey or if you're playing a role to help someone as a parent/guardian, peer coach, manager, HR director, business owner, etc., everyone needs tools. Please visit our website and peruse our tools, which we plan to continue to add on a regular basis. Please visit *www.jamesrosseausr.com*

Thought of the day

As I mentioned in the book, I invite you to sign up and receive the Thought of the Day each morning. It might just be the jump start you need for your day! Visit *www.jamesrosseausr.com* and sign up.